Anonymous

A History of the Celebration of Robert Burns' 110th Natal Day,

at the Metropolitan Hotel, New York

Anonymous

A History of the Celebration of Robert Burns' 110th Natal Day,
at the Metropolitan Hotel, New York

ISBN/EAN: 9783337419172

Printed in Europe, USA, Canada, Australia, Japan

Cover: Foto ©ninafisch / pixelio.de

More available books at **www.hansebooks.com**

A HISTORY

OF THE

CELEBRATION OF ROBERT BURNS'

110th NATAL DAY,

AT THE METROPOLITAN HOTEL.

NEW YORK.

———— •+• ————

JERSEY CITY:
PRINTED BY JOHN H. LYON

————

1869

Officers.

Members.

A

University of the State of New York

Charter of

Seneca Falls Historical Society

WHEREAS a petition for incorporation by the University has been duly received containing satisfactory statements under oath as to the objects, plans, property and provisions for maintenance of the proposed corporation

THEREFORE being satisfied that all requirements prescribed by law or University ordinance for such an Asssociation have been fully met and that public interests justify such action, the regents by virtue of the authority conferred on them by law hereby incorporate

Harrison Chamberlain,	E. William Medden,	Albert W. Golder,
Hermon A. Carmer,	Belle Teller,	Janet Cowing,
Sheldron F. Frazier,	H. Grant Person,	Lillias R. Sanford.

and their successors in office under the corporate name of Seneca Falls His torical Society.

This Corporation shall be located at Seneca Falls, Seneca County, New York.

Its first trustees shall be the nine incorporators above named

Its object shall be the study of local and general history and the acquire- ment and preservation of papers and other articles of local historical interest and the territory of its principal work shall be Seneca County.

IN WITNESS WHEREOF the Regents grant this charter No 1669 under seal of the University, at the Cap-

[SEAL]   itol in Albany, June 27, 1904

A. S. DRAPER,

Recorded and took effect 3:45 p. m , June 27, 1904   Com. of Education

B

Index.

Centennial Anniversary of Seneca County.

The Centennial Anniversary of the formation of Seneca County was observed by the Seneca Falls Historical Society at a meeting in the Wesleyan Methodist church on Monday evening, March 21st, 1904. Harrison Chamberlain, president of the Society, presided and made the following address, after which he read Hon. Diedrich Willers historical sketch of the formation of the county:

ADDRESS BY HARRISON CHAMBERLAIN.

To build up a commonwealth is a noble endeavor. To lay the foundations deep and strong, so joining communities and counties together that the structure will be harmonious and serve the public good is a task so patriotic, wise and grand that it confers on all taking a part in it an imperishable glory.

The formation of Seneca county was in line of State-building, of readjusting conditions the better to meet the needs of an increasing population. And how well this adjustment was made is evidenced by the fact that we are assembled here to-day to commemorate its centennial anniversary, and draw inspiration from the lives of those who wrought it.

I want to speak for a few moments of the men of 1804. On this occasion they deserve our meed of praise. They were of a sturdy, heroic race, coming here, influenced by not the Spanish greed for gain, not to ravage the country of its wealth and leave it despoiled and barren. Rather they came to give of themselves, to build up homes, to cultivate the soil and utilize the forests and enrich the land by their skill and energy. They were builders of settlements, able to conceive and execute great enterprises, shrinking from no hardships and fearing no dangers. Simple in habits and wanting maybe the social polish of to-day they possessed elements that imparted to them strong personality. They stood foremost in their place, impressing those about them with their strong, manly qualities. They were looked up to and their opinions went unquestioned; their advice was sought and confidently followed. Exact in their ideas of life their conceptions of duty were as precise as their practice of it was rigid and severe. The home had its rules and though these were strict and unyielding they were cheerfully complied with. In social and business relations there was a like preciseness of uprightness and integrity expected and demanded of all. Mingling with and softening these features was a kind and generous disposition. It would be difficult to find examples of kind and unselfish deeds to match the generous and ready service that the early settler was quick to extend to his neighbor. If one were in distress for food the fact was known and the best of the most fortunate was poured out. If a house or barn were to be raised the neighbors laid aside their work and came to the raising. If the hay or grain were to be cut and garnered and the farmer for any reason was unable to do it those in the vicinity came generous

2

ly to his assistance. Everyone felt in
close touch with his neighbor, though
miles might separate their homes, felt
a keen sense of dependence and was
moved by a common sympathy that
drew families together and created a
common brotherhood.

The men of 1804 were of strong conviction and purpose. Indeed there
was no place in the conditions of life
for the weakling and vacillating. In
the mode of training the young, consti-
tutional defects were largely elimi-
nated. The tasks imposed created
strong bodies and hardened muscle,
the responsibility imparted confidence
and courage, nourished a strong mental
fibre and fitted the young to take their
station in life. In this regimen there
was a Spartan spirit, seeking the best
and strongest in character. And as
you read of the men of 1804 in this
light you see in the circumstances surrounding them the forces of denial and
sacrifice that made them strong of
mind and will and enabled them to
achieve great deeds.

In the distant view there is a beauty
that is apt to disappear upon closer ap-
proach. Are we ascribing virtues to
the men of 1804 that they did not pos-
sess? Have their deeds by an inverse
rule enlarged as we recede from them?
We think not. The judgement of history has confirmed their worth. Faults
they had, but virtues greater and more
enduring. In their veins flowed the
blood of the Puritan, of the Dutch and
Huguenot, a strain of the most aggres-
sive in thought and action, imbued
with a love for freedom and emphasized
by an ancestry that had battled for
more than two centuries for conscience
and liberty. Here they came from
the fields of New England, from Manhattan island and the Keystone State,
drawn not more by our fertile soils
than by the liberal policy of the State
that offered settlers the greatest freedom and material advantages. Here
was the first West; here the first field
of action and enterprise; here was a
liberty associated with the finest opportunity of acquiring an ample and
independent fortune. Here they lived
and toiled; here they planted free institutions and laid the foundation of a
commonwealth that in three generations has made the State of New York
rank the first in the Union.

Men of 1804! We pay you honor!
We wreath a garland for you.

"As we walk to-day the halls of story,
  Mid pictures of the olden time,
And voices from an ancient glory,
  That charm us like a silver chime.
    The old and new join loving hands,
    The past before the present stands;
The ages give each other greeting,
  And years recall their old renown,
Their deeds of chivalry repeating,
  That won for them their golden crown."

Seneca County.

An Historical Address by Hon. Diedrich Willers of Varick, N. Y.

"Our Father's God from out whose hand,
The centuries fall like grains of sand,
We meet to-day united, free,
And loyal to our land and Thee,
To think Thee for the era done,
And trust Thee for the opening one "

MR. PRESIDENT, LADIES AND GENTLE-
MEN:—We have assembled here (under
the auspices of the Seneca Falls Historical society) to commemorate the
one hundredth anniversary of the official organization of the county of Seneca from territory of Cayuga county,
to take a retrospective survey of the
century past, and to seek therefrom,
lessons for guidance in the future.

The consideration of a subject so
vast and far reaching as this historical
review, covering an entire century,
within the time allotted to me, calls
for only a general statement and avoid-
ing of detail relating to the several
towns.

The first white men to penetrate the
wilderness region, covered by this
county, were missionaries, prompted
by no sordid motives, but solely with
self-sacrificing zeal, to labor for the
spiritual welfare of the Indians. Of
these, the earliest were Jesuit missionaries, who in the period 1656 to 1684
established mission stations among the
Cayuga nation of Indians—one called
St. Stephen at the Indian village (Tiohero) situate on the east side of Cayuga outlet (Seneca river), a short distance from the north end of Cayuga
lake, and another one at St. Rene
(Onontare), near the present village of
Savannah, in the bounds of the old
town of Galen, and near the north line
of the present county of Seneca. The
ministrations of these missionaries extended also to the Indians residing on
both sides of Cayuga lake and to the
Seneca tribe of Indians further west.

The devoted Moravian missionaries,
Bishop Cammerhoff and Rev. David
Zeisberger, visited the Onondagas and
also the Cayugas at the principal town
of the latter, near Union Springs, on
he east side of Cayuga lake, which

they crossed and then passed on foot
over the territory of this county in
1750, upon a spiritual mission to the
Seneca Indians—returning by the same
route after a short absence. Rev.
Samuel Kirkland, who served as a missionary to the Seneca Indians at Kanadesega (near Geneva) in 1765-66, passed up Seneca river in a batteaux, across
this county. In his ministrations to
the Senecas he sometimes also visited
the east side of Seneca lake.

A few traders with the Indians were
also early visitors between the Cayuga
and Seneca lakes prior to the American
revolution. The military expedition
of General John Sullivan, in 1779, during a trying period of the Revolutionary war, to chastise the hostile Indians
of Western New York, proved to be of
great importance to this locality. We
need not recount in detail the onward
march of the expedition, or its several
movements from Easton, Pennsylvania.

Leaving Elmira (Kanawaholla) after
a decisive battle with the Indians, the
army reached the east side of Seneca
lake, in the present town of Hector,
September 3d, and continued to march
northward, destroying the Indian village of Kendaia September 5th, and
rescuing Luke Swetland, who had resided there a year as an Indian captive.
Continuing its march, the command
reached and forded the outlet of Seneca
lake at its northeast corner and arrived
at Kanadesega (near Geneva) on the
7th of September. The expedition then
advanced through the Seneca Indian
territory to the Genesee river, carrying
destruction in its path, and returned to
Geneva by September 19th. The main
army began its return march south-
ward, September 20th, upon the east
side of Seneca lake. On the same day
detachments under Col. William Butler
and Col. Peter Gansevoort marched
eastward on the north side of Seneca
river, completing the destruction of
the Indian village of Skoiyase, upon

the site of the present village of Waterloo (which had already been visited and partly destroyed on September 8th by a detachment under command of Col John Harper), and encamped there for the night. Resuming their march on the next day, the detachments marched across the locality of the present town of Seneca Falls, to the outlet of Cayuga lake, a short distance north from the lake and near the Indian village of Tiohero (St Stephen) on the east side. Fording the outlet, the command of Col. Gansevoort proceeded to Albany and Col Butler marched up the east shore of Cayuga lake, destroying several Indian villages and proceeding to Elmira, rejoined the main army near there, on September 28th.

On September 21st, Col Henry Dearborn with a detachment of 200 men, after leaving the main army, marched across Fayette to Cayuga lake and destroyed three Indian villages on the west shore of Cayuga lake, near Canoga, and proceeded south along the west shore, destroying several additional villages and rejoined the main army near Elmira, on September 26th.

The chastisement of the hostile Indians was indeed severe, but paved the way to peace and to the relinquishment of their lands and their occupation by early settlers.

General Sullivan and his army were much surprised to find on all sides evidences of great fertility of soil and beauty of location, in the lake region of Western New York, in which are found the "Finger lakes" so called.

In their devastating march through the Indian country large quantities of corn, beans, melons, etc., were either consumed or destroyed; also an abundance of apples, plums and peaches.

The soldiers on their return home, gave glowing accounts of the "Lake region," which soon after became known as the "Genesee country," and some of the pioneer settlers of this county were soldiers who had marched with the army across this locality in 1779.

Elkanah Watson of Albany, N. Y., who was interested in lands in this locality, and who made a trip here in September, 1791, in writing of the Lake country, said: "The map of the world does not exhibit, in any other country, two lakes equal in magnitude to the Seneca and Cayuga, which are so singularly and happily situated. What a theme for poets, painters, philosophers and travelers, for the last two thousand years, had they been found in Italy! In general, the country lying between these beautiful lakes, rises gradually in symmetry from the opposite shores toward the center, producing a pleasing effect. Whenever it reaches a cultivated state, by the vigorous arm of freemen, it will become the 'Paradise of America.'" The poet, James G. Percival, has written of the beauties of Seneca lake, and a member of your Historical society, has written a "Sonnet to Lake Cayuga."

Our narrative of events cannot, however, be confined to the exact limits of a century, but it must relate back to the first permanent settlements in this county, fifteen to seventeen years prior to its official organization.

It is indeed fitting that our meeting to-night should be held in the town in which the first location and the first settlement in this county were made in 1787.

When this first location was made, our territory was still a part of Montgomery county, and then passing through three changes in a decade, the county of Herkimer followed in 1791, Onondaga in 1794, and then our immediate parent —Cayuga county—was organized in 1799, a county which still retained a large area.

The position of Seneca county, as will be seen upon the State map, is a peculiar one—the lakes, Seneca and Cayuga, bordering its west and east shores, with the Seneca river running across the county from lake to lake, forms a part of it, into a peninsular shape.

The county seat of Cayuga county for a number of years after 1799 was somewhat fluctuating, but in order to reach either, Cayuga village, on the east shore of Cayuga lake, or Aurora, on the same side, in which villages the county business was transacted, the waters of Cayuga lake must be crossed, and although, after 1800, the Cayuga bridge, near the north end of the lake, one mile and eight rods in length, connected the present territory of Seneca county with Cayuga village, the village of Aurora could only be reached by small boats propelled by oarsmen or by small sailing vessels, or, indeed, by a circuitous overland route.

The difficult communication with Cayuga county, with county seat rivalries and the ambition of "local statesmen," were doubtless prominent causes for the organization of the county of Seneca. When the question of the formation of a new county was first agitated in 1802 several projects were discussed. One of these was for a division of Cayuga county east and west, by a line commencing at Seneca lake and running east on the line between Romulus and Ovid, crossing Cayuga lake and the military townships of Scipio and Sempronius, to the county of Onondaga. The territory north of this line and continuing the entire width of Cayuga county to Lake Ontario, to constitute one county (doubtless to remain as Cayuga county), and that part of the territory of Cayuga county as then constituted, lying south of the above line to constitute another county, probably the new one. It is said, that had Cayuga county been divided by an east and west line as above, that the county seat of the north county would have been established at Cayuga bridge and of the south county at Ithaca, in the town of Ulysses.

A second project was for a north and south division, substantially the same as the one adopted by the Legislature in 1804 in the formation of Seneca county.

Still another project is indicated in a petition presented to the Assembly by William Powell and others of Ontario county, praying that a part of Ontario county and a part of Cayuga county be formed into a new county. The Assembly Journal does not show the precise plan, but it probably contemplated the erection of a new county by a north and south division of Cayuga, and the annexation of Geneva and vicinity thereto.

The question of dividing Cayuga county was brought before the State Legislature of 1803, when petitions in favor thereof were presented to the State Senate, and on March 16th of that year, Senator Lemuel Chipman of Ontario county, brought in a bill to

give effect to the prayer of the petitioners. The bill was read twice and committed to the committee of the whole, but no further action was taken thereon by the legislature in that year. In 1804, however, the division question took active form and a number of petitions favoring the several projects, and several remonstrances, were introduced in both houses of the Legislature.

Dr. Silas Halsey, a resident in the bounds of the present town of Lodi, then Ovid, had, while a resident there, been elected to the State Legislature, as a Member of Assembly from Onondaga county for the years 1797 and 1798, and again represented Cayuga county as its first Member of Assembly in 1800 and was continued in 1801, 1803 and 1804 from that county.

During this long term of legislative service, Doctor Halsey had become well versed in legislation and had formed an extensive acquaintance at Albany, so that his efforts in behalf of the new county were of great value to the friends of that project, although Cayuga in 1803-4 had three Members of Assembly, of whom two resided east of Cayuga lake.

Joseph Annin, a resident in the present territory of Cayuga county, was one of the Senators from the Western district of this State, and the immediate representative of Cayuga county in the State Senate in 1803-4.

It is not positively known whether Assemblyman Halsey and Senator Annin both favored the same division project. However, on February 3d, 1804, when a petition was presented in the Assembly by citizens of the town of Hector, praying that the territory situate between Cayuga and Seneca lakes, etc., be erected into a new county. It was referred to a special committee of five, of which Dr. Halsey was named chairman.

On February 27th of the same year, Dr. Halsey introduced "an act to divide the county of Cayuga and for other purposes," which was read twice and referred to the committee of the whole. On March 7th the bill was favorably considered, and on March 9th referred to a select committee of which Dr. Halsey was chairman to report complete. He reported back the bill with amendments, which were agreed to, and on March 10th it passed the Assembly. The Senate, after consideration, passed the Assembly bill without amendment on March 21st, and it received the approval Governor George Clinton on March 24th, 1804, and became a law on that day. The name "Seneca" given to the new county—as well as the name of Seneca lake and Seneca river—is derived from the Seneca nation of Indians, the strongest and most warlike tribe of the Six Nations or Iroquois Indians.

The exact boundary line between the lands of the Cayuga and Seneca nations of Indians was not very closely defined, and as late as December, 1789, an agreement was entered into with this State, whereby the Seneca nation agreed to the old Pre emption line running a little west of Geneva, and north to Lake Ontario, as a boundary line, and conceding to the Cayugas the whole of Great Sodus bay, known as "Bay of the Cayugas." The whole of Seneca lake, however, belonged to the Seneca nation, and it is said that a few fishing villages on its east side, near its north end, belonged to the same nation, together with the Indian village of Kendaia. All the rest of the present Seneca county, it is believed, belonged to the Cayuga Indians. Our county, therefore, while receiving the name "Seneca," was really a part of the original domain of the Cayugas, and it was the fourth county to be named from an Iroquois tribe—Onondaga, Oneida and Cayuga having preceded it.

The county of Seneca, by the act of incorporation of 1804 embraced a territory described as follows: The south boundary, beginning at the head of Seneca lake, at the southwest corner of the town of Hector—thence running east on the south line of the towns of Hector and Ulysses, to the southeast corner of the last named town (the whole of the town of Ulysses and Hector being included in Seneca county—and the south boundary of Ulysses extending about 4½ miles south of Ithaca) The east boundary, being constituted by the town of Dryden and the center of Cayuga lake, and its outlet, to the west line of the town of Brutus, and thence north in the west line of Brutus and Cato, and farther on north to Lake

Ontario—the north boundary extending along Ontario lake to the county of Ontario, thence south along the Ontario county or new Pre-emption line to Seneca lake. The west boundary, which has been the subject of considerable comment and controversy, had been already defined in the boundaries of Cayuga county, established by the Revised Laws of 1801, (and continued as to Seneca county in the Revised Laws of 1813)—as bounded westerly by the line called the new Pre-emption line, from Lake Ontario to Seneca lake and thence along the west shore of said lake to the southwest corner of the township of Hector.

After the counties of Tompkins and Wayne had been erected, in part from Seneca county, the Revised Statutes passed in 1827, describe the county boundaries as they now exist, as follows: All that part of the State bounded on the north by the county of Wayne, on the east by the county of Cayuga, on the south by the county of Tompkins (and now in part belonging to Schuyler county) and on the west by the west shore of the Seneca lake, and from the north end of said lake, by the Pre emption line, as established by law.

The territory of the new county, in 1804, comprised lands in the Military tract, Cayuga reservations and the Williamson Compensation Patent, (at the north end), situate in the six towns of Ovid, Romulus, Junius and Fayette, with Hector and Ulysses.

The county extended in length, north and south, sixty three miles with an average width of eleven miles and an area of 744 square miles, or 476,160 acres of land.

One hundred years ago, when Seneca county was organized, its population was sparse and some of its territory, especially at the extreme north end, was almost an unbroken forest!

The Indian ownership of the West Cayuga reservation had not been ceded and relinquished until 1795, and a Cayuga Sachem, Fish Carrier, was still interested in a reservation at Canoga. Our pioneer settlers, not infrequently met Indians, and as late as 1803, one of the early settlers in the bounds of the present town of Tyre, was murdered by an Indian, although to the credit of both pioneers and Indians, it may be said, that they usually maintained friendly relations.

The population of the original territory included in Seneca county by the U. S. Census of 1890, was only 4,984, divided as follows: Ovid, including Hector, 2,169; Romulus, 1,025; Fayette, including Junius and the entire north end of county to Lake Ontario, 863, and Ulysses 927. The town of Ovid, included the center of population of this territory.

It is not our purpose, to enter at length into the history of the settlement of the several towns, as to which there is some dispute, as to priority. As already stated, Seneca Falls contained the earliest settlement by Job Smith in 1787, followed by Lawrence Van Cleef and others, in 1789. Romulus, Ovid, Lodi and Waterloo were also settled in 1789, while the other towns of the present county, followed within a few years later. The town of Ulysses, claims settlement in 1789, and Hector in 1791, while the towns of Galen and Wolcott, which formed a part of our original county (although not yet organized at the time of its formation), were not settled until 1800 and afterward.

It has been well said, "that the founders of every community, impress their characteristics, which remain fixed for a long period, perhaps permanently."

The early settlers of Seneca county represented German and Scotch Irish from Pennsylvania, Holland Dutch and English from New Jersey and Eastern New York, Yankees from the New England States, with a few persons of foreign birth. From such an admixture, including many Revolutionary soldiers, a conservative, industrious, frugal, and patriotic population has resulted.

Usually, in the formation of a new county, there is a contest, upon the location of the county buildings, and the legislation which provides for their location, is sometimes very shrewdly drawn, to accomplish a desired purpose.

The act for organization of Seneca county, required the supervisors of the new county, to raise one thousand dollars for buildings, and named John Sayre of Romulus, James VanHorne of

Ovid and Grover Smith of Hector, as a commission to superintend the building of a court house and jail, "to be erected in the town of Ovid, and not more than four miles south of the north line of said town, and not less than three miles from the Seneca and Cayuga lakes." It was further provided, that the courts for the county "shall be holden at the meeting house on Lot No 30 in the town of Ovid," undoubtedly the first church edifice erected in the bounds of the present county—about five miles southeast of Ovid village—until further legislation; also, that prisoners be confined in jail at Elmira, until county jail is completed.

The commissioners, it will be seen, were really restricted as to the location of the site, between the North boundary of the town of Ovid, and a line extending south four miles, reaching to the present town of Lodi, and three miles east of Seneca lake.

The village of Lancaster, situate upon the site of the present village of Willard, in the town of Romulus, desired the location of the county seat, and at a special town meeting, held in that town, June 9th, 1804, its citizens protested vigorously against this location and the town of Washington (Fayette), in special town meeting held July 7th in the same year, took similar adverse action.

It is understood that the town of Ulysses, in which the promising village of Ithaca was located, was also decidedly opposed to the proposed location of the county buildings, as were also the inhabitants of Junius.

The first board of supervisors of the new county, which convened at Ovid, October 2d, 1804, and adjourned to the house of John McMath, about two miles south of the village, refused, at first, by a tie vote, to appropriate moneys for erecting county buildings, the supervisors of Ovid, Hector and Romulus voting in the affirmative, and the supervisors of Junius, Fayette and Ulysses, voting in the negative. Before adjournment, however, the sum of one thousand dollars was appropriated, leaving the question as to location of site of the county buildings, open to further legislation.

The legislature of 1805, refused to change the location, but made it still more definite and positive, by requiring the building commissioners to locate the county buildings, on lot No. 3, (upon the site of Ovid village) the site to be located not exceeding fifty rods west of the three mile limit from Seneca lake, imposed in the preceding year. From this, it is evident, that some measurement had been made during the year, showing that the desired site was not quite three miles from Seneca lake. It may be added here, that as early as 1797, when the territory of this county, still formed a part of Onondaga county, the courts of that county were required by the legislature to be held, at Manlius, Aurora and at the house of Andrew Dunlap in Ovid. The Ovid term to be held on the 4th Tuesday of September.

Hon. John Delafield, in his county history says, that this term of court was held at the barn of Andrew Dunlap. At the session of the legislature in 1805 it was provided that the court appointed to be held at the meeting house, already referred to, on the second Tuesday of May 1805, after convening, shall adjourn to the house of John Seeley on Lot 3 aforesaid. Through the courtesy of County Clerk Savage, it has been ascertained, that the site for county buildings at Ovid, on Lot 3 aforesaid, was deeded to the supervisors of the county of Seneca, by John Seeley and wife, by an absolute deed of conveyance, for a "consideration of five dollars, and the advantages and emoluments arising from the building of a court house." The site comprises three acres of land, including the public park in front of the buildings. The erection of the court house and jail, was begun in 1806, and completed without delay, and thus the machinery of the new county was fully set in operation, Dr. Silas Halsey having been appointed county clerk.

As indicating the influence of the towns of Hector and Ulysses in the affairs of the new county, it may be mentioned, that the first sheriff appointed in 1804, was a resident of Hector, and the appointee for first judge of the Court of Common Pleas, was a resident of Ulysses, as were also his two successors, and up to 1815, this important office was held by a resident of Ulysses. Hon. Cornelius Humfrey,

the first appointee for judge, was also elected supervisor of Ulysses in 1805, although later a resident of Hector. Five residents of Ulysses also served as Members of Assembly, during the thirteen year period before the erection, of Tompkins county, and one Representative in Congress, Dr. Oliver C. Comstock, for four years. For a number of years, the public affairs of the county, now seemingly moved along smoothly. The town of Wolcott, adjoining Lake Ontario, was erected a town in 1807, although not fully organized and represented in our board of supervisors until 1810. In 1812, that town was however annexed to Cayuga county, and remained in connection with that county, until 1817, when it was re-annexed to Seneca county.

The town of Galen was organized in 1812, from territory lying on the north of Junius. The population of the south towns increased most rapidly, and the inhabitants of Ulysses becoming more and more restive, sought the erection of a new county, with county seat at Ithaca.

For several years prior to 1817, one of the Members of Assembly from Seneca county, had been elected from Ulysses, and in the last named year, Hon. Archer Green was one of the Representatives from this county.

The influence of Hon. Simeon DeWitt, a resident of Ithaca, and for fifty years surveyor general of this State at Albany, then in active public life, had been exerted for a new county, with county buildings at Ithaca, to secure which, he and other citizens made liberal offers. Hon. Elisha Williams, a property holder at Waterloo, represented Columbia county in the Assembly for several years, including the year 1817.

The county of Seneca was in 1817 represented in the State Senate by Hon. John Knox of Waterloo, who favored the new county, and although Hon. Wm. Thompson of Ovid, was a Member of Assembly that year, the combined influence of Waterloo and Ithaca, was too great for him to overcome, and on April 7th, 1817, the new county of Tompkins was erected, which included the towns of Hector and Ulysses, from Seneca county. Not content with the annexation of these towns, the new town of Covert erected from Ovid on the same day, extending from lake to lake, was also annexed to the new county, leaving Ovid only four miles from the south line of the county.

It may be here stated, that two years afterwards, by act of April 13th, 1819, the town of Covert was re-annexed to Seneca county, and Ovid was then located nine miles from the south line of the county.

The Act erecting Tompkins county, named Hon. John Knox, and Reuben Swift of Waterloo and John Watkins of South Waterloo, as building commissioners to erect court house and jail for Seneca county, on a site at Waterloo to be conveyed to the county. The act required the supervisors to raise four thousand dollars in aid of erecting the new buildings, whenever the building commissioners certified that a like amount had been voluntarily contributed.

The site for the county buildings was as the county clerk states, conveyed by absolute deed of conveyance, on July 4th, 1817, to the supervisors of Seneca county by Hon. Elisha Williams of Hudson, N. Y., and Reuben Swift and wife of Waterloo, the consideration named in deed, being "one dollar, and the advantages arising from the building of a court house at Waterloo."

The building commissioners reported to the board of supervisors in October 1817, that four thousand dollars had been raised by voluntary contributions and requested a like appropriation from the county. This request was denied, as were several motions to raise lesser amounts, but finally before the board adjourned, the sum of five hundred dollars was voted.

The buildings were erected in 1818, and in compliance with the terms of the act, Waterloo became the sole county seat.

The village of Ovid and the south towns of the county, while losing the county seat, were undismayed, perhaps little thinking that in six years, Waterloo, would by the erection of another new county, be placed in precisely the same position, as that of Ovid in 1817. The legislature was again appealed to for relief, and in 1822, when Hon John Maynard, at that time a resident of Ovid, represented Seneca county as

Member of Assembly, with Hon. James Dickson of Galen, by Act chapter 137 laws of that year, the county was divided into two jury districts, by the south line of Fayette, a division in effect creating north and south jury districts, which still exists, and requiring the courts to be held alternately in the same, and also providing for the use of jails at Waterloo and Ovid. The passage of this act, created substantially the half shire system of court houses, which the creation of a new county, the following year, cemented more strongly. The Act of 1822, also provided, "that it shall not be lawful for the supervisors to sell the court house in Ovid, or the land on which the same stands."

When the construction of the Erie canal was authorized in 1817, it crossed the town of Galen, in the territory of which, several important villages were located. A movement for a new county culminated in 1823, when Hon. Ananias Wells of Galen was one of the Members of Assembly from Seneca county and Hon. Byram Green of Sodus, then in Ontario county, was a member of the State Senate. By Act Chapter 138, Laws of 1823, passed April eleventh, in that year, the county of Wayne was erected, and the towns of Galen and Wolcott were annexed thereto, the large area of these two towns now forming six towns of that county. Ovid and Wayne county, evidently joined forces, this time against Waterloo. The two towns annexed, embraced all of the territory of Seneca county north of Junius and left Waterloo village, only eight miles from the north boundary of the county.

Although efforts were made in 1844 and 1854 in the board of supervisors to secure a single set of centrally located county buildings at Bearytown, the project was lost in 1854, by one vote less than the necessary two thirds vote (the vote resulting six ayes and four noes) and the half shire system with two jury districts established in 1822, and perpetuated in 1823, still remains in full force and effect. The rotation system, in nominations for county officers, between the towns of the two jury districts long practised by the two leading political parties, has of late years not been closely observed. The number of towns had now become reduced to five, Ovid, Romulus, Fayette, Junius and Covert, to which Lodi was added in 1826, Seneca Falls, Waterloo and Tyre in 1829, and Varick in 1830, making the number ten, as now existing. No change in the towns has been made since, and no change in town territory, except, two slight changes in Ovid boundaries in the year 1837 and 1843. There are now four incorporated villages in the county, Waterloo, Seneca Falls, Ovid and Farmer, the latter dating from 1904.

The area of the county as now reduced, extended thirty-two miles north and south in length, and an average width of about ten miles and contains 199,500 acres of land, the two court houses being situate fitteen miles apart in a direct line. In order to complete the statement relating to county buildings it may be added here that the Board of Supervisors has from time to time, since 1823, maintained and improved the county buildings at Waterloo and Ovid.

A proposition to rebuild the court house at Ovid failed in 1841 and 1843. but was adopted by the board in 1844, the contract was let therefor and the building completed upon the lot where the first court house had been located. The county clerk's office at Ovid was authorized to be built in 1859 and completed by 1861.

The erection of a county clerk's office at Waterloo was authorized in 1858 59, and completed in 1861. the land therefor having been conveyed to the County in the latter year. The building and lot were ordered sold by the Supervisors in December, 1900. and the erection of a new county clerk's office, to include also surrogate's office was provided for, adjoining the court house, and which was completed for occupancy early in the year 1902. The present jail at Waterloo was authorized to be built in 1866 and completed the next year.

It may be of interest to note the several attempts since 1817, to change the court house site, and boundaries of Seneca County, as well as annexation schemes. After the erection of Tomp-

kins County and during the controversy between Waterloo and Ovid over the county buildings, already in 1818, no tice of application to the legislature of 1819 was published, asking for the annexation to Seneca County of the town of Seneca (including Geneva) and the town of Phelps, Ontario County, with half shire court houses at Waterloo and Geneva. This application failed. In 1829, several years after the erection of Wayne county, an application was made to the legislature for a new county to comprise the five north towns of Seneca County and the towns of Phelps and Seneca in Ontario County with half shire court house at Waterloo and Geneva. This application also failed.

The question of division or annexation was discussed from time to time, but in 1869, when Judge Charles J. Folger, of Geneva, held a seat in the state senate, it again took such formidable shape that a special meeting of the Board of Supervisors of this County was held on February 18th of that year, at which your honored townsman, Hon. Gilbert Wilcoxen presided. and strong resolutions were adopted, reciting:

"WHEREAS, An effort is being made to annex the towns of Seneca and Phelps in the County of Seneca, to the County of Seneca, making Geneva the county seat of the proposed county, therefore

Resolved, That in the opinion of this board such a measure is inexpedient, unwise and uncalled for by any public necessity of the County of Seneca, and is, we believe, entirely opposed to the wishes of a very large majority of the people of this county. On calling the ayes and nayes the preamble and resolution was adopted by nine ayes, one nay. (the Supervisor of Lodi.) It was further

Resolved, That we do earnestly protest against any change in the boundaries of Seneca County, as at present organized." This resolution was adopted by eight affirmative votes, two votes being cast in the negative (the Supervisors of Lodi and Junius.) This scheme again failed and let us hope that the sentiment of fidelity to this county expressed in this resolution may long continue to prevail therein.

The latest project for change embraced the annexation of the city of Geneva to Seneca County or the annexation of Border City in the town of Waterloo, to Geneva. The Board of Supervisors of this County at its annual session in 1902, on December 19th, adopted the following resolution:

"*Resolved*, that a committee of three be appointed by the chairman to act in thematter regarding the annexation of Geneva to Seneca County or the annexation of Border City to Geneva." A committee was appointed to look after and oppose this change. This scheme, like its predecessors, was unsuccessful. The Supervisors in 1903, however, again appointed a committee to guard the interests of this County.

The population of the original territory of Seneca County in 1800, has been already stated. In 1810, it had increased to 16,609, in 1814 to 21,401. Even after the annexation of two large towns to Tompkins county, it reached 23,619, in 1820, and in 1825 after the erection of Wayne County, and the loss of two more towns, leaving the county area, as at present, it was 20,-169. The greatest population attained by the county at any time, was 28,138 in 1860, since which time the population of six towns has decreased, and notwithstanding the increase in population of Seneca Falls and Waterloo and the increase since the opening of Willard State Hospital in 1869, in Ovid and Romulus—the population by the census of 1900, was 28,114

Based upon population, from 1804 to 1815 inclusive, the county elected one Member of Assembly; in 1816 and 1817, three members; from 1818 to 1836 inclusive, two members; and since the latter date, one member

The tendency of population to large villages and cities, and the falling off in population of agricultural towns—on account of consolidation of farms, etc., causes which affect many other counties of the state, sufficiently accounts for the falling off in our population, without assigning other causes.

Our county has reached and passed a number of important periods or epochs, in its process of development, from the time of the earliest settlements made within its borders. A few of these will be mentioned:

1. The opening of the Bennett-Harris ferry across Cayuga Lake, and the first State Road crossing thereat, 1790-1791 followed by the Great Genesee road 1796-97, both leading from the eastern part of the state to Geneva, and farther west, and the incorporation of the Seneca Turnpike Road Company, 1800-1801.

2. The opening of the famous Cayuga Bridge across Cayuga Lake in 1800, and the impetus given to travel and the carrying of United States mails by the organization of lines of stages.

3. The incorporation of the Ithaca and Geneva Turnpike Company in 1810, and its partial completion for travel and transportation of the United States mails.

4. The improvement of the navigation of the Seneca river and other early improvements, by the Seneca Lock Navigation company, 1813 1819.

5. The opening for traffic of the Erie Canal from Albany to Montezuma and its completion in 1825, followed by the Cayuga and Seneca canal completed in 1828 and the new method of travel by canal packet boats.

6 The opening of steamboat travel and traffic on Cayuga lake (1820) and on Seneca lake (1828).

7. The opening for travel and business of the Auburn and Rochester railroad across this county in 1841, making a continuous line of railroad to Albany.

8 The establishment of telegraph and telephone lines and of express offices.

9. The completion of a line of the Geneva Ithaca & Sayre railroad, (now Lehigh Valley) across this county in 1873, and of a second line in 1892, with a branch to Seneca Falls in 1898.

10 The development of manufactories in the villages of Seneca Falls, Waterloo, Farmer Village and other villages of the county.

11. Improved methods of farming and introduction of improved machinery connected therewith.

12. The opening of an electric line of railway across the county to Cayuga Lake Park with promise of further extension.

Time will not permit an extended notice of public schools and teachers, or of educational progress in this county.

When the first general act for the encouragement of public schools was passed in 1795, there were very few schools within our boundaries, and these were privately supported. Under the act, a number of schools were established but it was not until after the passage of an act by the state legislature in 1812 for the organization and establishment of common schools, that school districts were systematically organized and established.

The state, at an early date, made small appropriations for public schools and these were aided in the towns of the military tract, by income from the gospel and school lot.

An application to the state school department for information as to schools in this county as early as 1804, elicited the response that the department has no record of Seneca County school districts prior to 1838.

Spafford's Gazetteer of the state of New York, published in 1813, mentions thirty three school houses in the towns of Ovid, Romulus and Fayette, by the census of 1810, but gives no data as to the other towns, and it is safe to give the number at that time, as fifty. This was the era of log school houses, followed by the "little red school house," and within the past sixty years, by commodious and well adapted structures. In 1838, there were in the bounds of the present county, 116 school districts, which number has become reduced by the consolidation of districts, and the formation of several Union High schools, to ninety-two school districts in 1903.

Academies were established and incorporated at Ovid in 1830, at Seneca Falls in 1837 and at Waterloo in 1842. All of these academic institutions are now continued as Union High schools, and in addition, a high school has been established at the village of Farmer.

The Seneca Falls Union High school is still known as Mynderse Academy, in honor of its early patron, Col. Wilhelmus Mynderse.

In 1853, the State Agricultural College was incorporated and located upon the farm of Hon John Delafield in Fayette, who was chosen its president. After his death, it was removed to Ovid, a college building was erected, and opened in 1860, under the presidency of Gen. Marsena R. Patrick, who retired therefrom to enter service in the Civil War.

This college was subsequently removed to Havana, Schuyler county, and afterwards to Ithaca, where having received the college land grant from the United States, it is now located as a Department of Cornell University. The only consolation for the diversion of this institution from Seneca county is, that it is now located in the original territory of Seneca County, and that the president of its Agricultural department, who long served in that capacity, was born in the present county.

The history of the State Agricultural College and Willard State Hospital,its success or, will be separately written and presented to your society, by one thoroughly conversant therewith.

The learned professions have been represented in this county by many prominent men.

At the time of the organization of the county, as far as can be ascertained there were only five organized religious congregations in the bounds of the present county, all at the south end, and two or three in Ulysses and Hector. With a single exception (the church on lot thirty, Ovid in which the first courts were held) it is believed that these congregations then worshipped in private houses, barns or school houses, and primitive log churches followed later, in some cases Some of these congregations were without regular pastors, and the first clergymen of the county, were those who officiated therein. Of these con gregations one in the town of Romulus, celebrated its centennial in 1895, one in Lodi in 1900, one in Varick, (at Romulus village) in 1902, and one each in Ovid and Covert, in 1903. During the next few years, one congregation in each of the towns of Fayette, Seneca Falls, Junius and Tyre, will attain one hundred years of age.

Many of the clergymen of this county, have enjoyed long pastorates, one at Bearytown for an active period of sixty years, one at Waterloo for thirty seven years, one at Romulus village f r twenty seven years, one at Ovid for twenty six years, one at Seneca Falls for twenty-one years, besides six or seven others, for periods of from fifteen to twenty years.

At the present time, the pastor of the Baptist church at Magee's Corners, in the town of Tyre (who is present with us to night) is serving his fortieth year in active ministry in the town in which he was born of patriotic Revolutionary ancestry.

There are at present forty-nine church edifices open for religious services in the county, besides several chapels (several rural churches having been closed) with forty pastors. These churches and chapels had by the last published census, a seating capacity for 20,850 persons. It is by no means a matter of which to be proud, but the truth of history compels the statement, that the Mormon church (called also the church of Latter Day Saints) was first organized in the town of Fayette, by Joseph Smith and five others, on April 6, 1830.

At the time of the organization of Seneca County, March 24, 1804, so far as has been ascertained, there was not a lawyer residing in the bounds of the present County, if indeed there were any such in the whole County as then existing. Many of the practising lawyers, from time to time, have taken a prominent and distinguished position at the Bar or on the Bench. The last ocurt calendar issued by the County Clerk, contains a roll of forty resident attorneys at law. The "Judiciary of Seneca County" is to be specially written up by one who will do full justice to the subject.

The medical profession has from the beginning been well represented. In the early history of the County, Dr. Silas Halsey served as member of assembly, the first county clerk, representative in Congress and in many other public capacities.

Dr. Jared Sandford served as the first surrogate and treasurer of the County; Dr. Oliver C. Comstock as judge, member of assembly and representative in Congress. Many other physicians have held prominent public positions and have enjoyed a high standing in their profession.

Dr. Alexander Coventry, who located with his family in Fayette in 1792, and afterwards removed to Oneida County, was twice elected president of the State Medical Society, and Dr. Henry D. Didama, a former resident of Romulus village, 1846 to 1851, now residing at Syracuse and serving as Dean of the Medical department of Syracuse University, at an advanced age, was honored with an election to the same position

Since the opening of Willard State Hospital for the insane, in 1869, the Medical Society of the County has been re inforced by a number of prominent physicians, whose labors in behalf of the unfortunates in their charge have been productive of much good. The history of this institution, one of the largest of its class in this state, shows an honorable and worthy record thoughout. It has at the present time, two thousand two hundred and twenty-five (2,225) patients.

The Editorial profession, the fourth estate, has been well sustained since the first newspaper was established at Ovid in 1815 At the present time six newspapers are published in the County, two at Seneca Falls, two at Waterloo and one each at Ovid and the village of Farmer. The newspapers of Seneca County have taken a deservedly high position in this state. One of the present editors has edited his newspaper in Seneca Falls for forty five years, and several others for more than an average period of editorial service. Several of the editors have been chosen to the highest positions in State Editorial Associations, of which they are honored members.

It has been said by a prominent statesman that "The cultivation of the soil is the foundation of all public prosperity." Farming has for many years been a leading pursuit in the County which has taken a high rank among the agricultural counties of this state.

The temperature of this county is favorably influenced by the waters of the adjacent lakes, which also exert a a genial influence upon the soil and its cultivation.

The aboriginal owners of the soil, recognized its fertility, even by the most primitive methods of cultivation.

Upon four occasions, the state premiums for the best farm in the state, has been awarded to farmers in this county, and on two occasions, the Presidency of the State Agricultural Society, has been given to farmers of Fayette. The distinguished honor conferred upon the county, when the first State Agricultural College was located therein, has been already mentioned.

Sixty years ago, wheat was the principal product. It is said that at one time in the decade between the years 1840 and 1850, the seven or eight flouring mills of Seneca Falls, in amount and value of manufactured products, ranked next in order to the fl uring mills of Oswego and Rochester.

It is to be regretted that farming has of late years been unremunerative, and that grape culture and fruit raising as adjuncts to farming have had much to contend with from severe winters, unfavorable seasons and insect enemies, so that farming lands have greatly depreciated in value.

The Patrons of Husbandry (or the Farmers Grange) have done much in the past thirty years, to elevate the standard of farming and to improve the condition of farmers and their families, as have also Farmers' Institutes held under the supervision of the State Commissioner of Agriculture.

In the early history of the county, its manufactured products and industries, were of the most primitive kinds.

These included the manufacture of potash, charcoal and maple sugar.

When the three flouring mills at South Waterloo, Lodi and Seneca Falls were completed, their respective proprietors, Samuel Bear, Dr. Silas Ha sey and Col. Wilhelmus Mynderse, were deemed the most public spirited, as well as popular men, in their several localities.

By far the most extensive system of manufacture, however, was that conducted in each well regulated family, in which linen and woolen fabrics, known as "home spun" were made for family use, by aid of spinning wheels and looms. The state census of 1810, reports the whole number of looms in families of this county, in that year as 601 producing fifty thousand yards of woolen c'oth, and 158,-000 yards of linen cloth. This manufacture also gave employment to seven fulling mills and ten carding machines. The census makes mention also of fifteen tanneries in the county in that year

In later years manufactures, especially those located upon the abundant water power of the Seneca river, have greatly prospered and have taken a high position. In order to do them justice and note their advancement from step to step, would require more time, than that allotted to me.

The traveller in other states and in foreign lands frequently sees the steam fire engine, and the various kinds of pumps and machinery, with other articles of manufacture from Seneca Falls, while the fabrics produced by the Woolen Mills of Seneca Falls and Waterloo, have a world wide reputation, and the musical instruments and vehicles manufactured at Waterloo, also the manufacture of Farmer, and other villages of the county, are well and favorably known, wherever introduced.

There is room for greater development and expansion in manufacture in our midst, to inure to the advantage not only of the manufacturer, but indeed to every one, for when the manufacturer and the farmer are prosperous every other pursuit and occupation is benefitted thereby.

The discovery and manufacture of salt, at and near the head of both Seneca and Cayuga Lakes, in adjoining counties recalls the fact, that before the settlement of this locality by white men, salt was found by the Indians, in this county on the west side of Cayuga Lake, near its foot, and in the town of Galen. It is believed that salt, will in time also be found along the shores of Seneca and Cayuga Lakes, in the towns of Lodi, Ovid and Covert, and thus add to the value of our manufactures.

The County records show that as early as February 12, 1805, a public library was organized in Ovid, known as Ovid Union library, and in the same year Seneca Library number one, located at Lancaster, in the town of Romulus, was organized. Both of these libraries have long since ceased to exist

The Waterloo Library and Historical Society was organized in 1875-76, and its library building completed in 1883. On September, 3, 1879, the centennial of General John Sullivan's Indian Expedition was successfully celebrated at Waterloo under its auspices, as was also the dedication of a monument to Red Jacket near Canoga, October 15, 1891. It has at present 7,441 volumes in its Library.

The Seneca Falls library was incorporated in 1892, and has already 4,198 volumes, although it has no permanent library building as yet.

The Seneca Falls Historical Society, separately organized about nine years ago, and incorporated 1904, has from the beginning devoted much attention to historical inquiry and research. It includes in its membership not only persons engaged in the learned professions but also business men in the several pursuits of life, and some of its most zealous and enthusiastic workers are ladies. In 1903, this society gave much attention to the commemoration of the centennial of the town of Junius. The present commemoration of the centennial of the official organization of Seneca County has engaged the attention of the society

for some time, and the collection and preservation of material connected therewith, will continue even after this meeting.

The Whittier library of Lodi, or ganized in August, 1898, has six hundred volumes in its library, and at the last town election the people of the town voted to extend financial aid in its behalf.

The Ovid library was organized December 21, 1899, and has already seven hundred volumes in its library.

A public library was also organized at Farmer, November 8, 1901, as the Farmer Free Library, and opened to the public July 22, 1905, which has six hundred and ten volumes on its shelves.

In the year 1838, the legislature of this state inaugurated a system of school district libraries. Many of the school districts accumulated several hundred volumes, and although some mistakes were made in selecting the same, many useful books were thus circulated in every neighborhood. In time the State reduced its appropriations for these libraries and school districts, diverted the same for other purposes, and books were lost also by locating libraries in school houses in some cases. The decline of the school district library is to be deeply regretted, and a re-establishment of the same, under suitable safeguards, would result in great advantage to every neighborhood.

In the treatment of our subject, we must occasionally present the dark as well as the bright side.

This County has its share of pauperism and crime and it cannot be denied that with increase of population there has been considerable increase in both, as well as in the expense of administration.

In the early years appropriations for the support of the poor were frequently voted at town meetings. The County poor house was opened for reception of poor persons in the year 1830, a farm having been purchased therefor by the county in that year, on the line of Fayette and Seneca Falls. The present poor house building, located in Fayette, was erected in 1853, and with internal changes, additions and improvements, is still in use. The number of permanent paupers therein has not greatly increased since the removal of the insane therefrom, but the number of temporary inmates has increased considerably in recent years, from the class known as pauper tramps. The cost of the poor administration in the several towns has been greatly increased, however, of late, by a somewhat liberal bestowment of temporary aid or out door relief

The passage of laws by the state legislature, forbidding the keeping of children over two years of age in the poor house, and the removal of all insane paupers therefrom to State hospitals for the insane, were measures which have commended themselves to all humanely disposed persons.

Already in the year 1803, the first murder was committed within the territory of the present County, then a part of Cayuga County, when Indian John, otherwise known as Delaware John, murdered Ezekiel Crane, a pioneer settler in the bounds of the present town of Tyre. In an historical paper on the "Early Records of Cayuga County," read before the Cayuga County Historical Society, by George W. Benham, Esq., county clerk, a former resident of Seneca Falls, he makes mention of the indictment and trial of the murderer. The indictment found bythe Grand Jury of Cayuga County is in the following words: "That John, a Delaware Indian, not having the fear of God before his eyes, but being moved and seduced by the instigation of the devil, on the 12th day of December, 1803, with a certain rifle gun, of the value of fifteen dollars, then and there loaded and charged with gun powder and one leaden bullet, did inflict a mortal wound of the depth of six inches, upon the person of Ezekiel Crane, of which wound said Ezekiel Crane died on the seventeenth day of December, 1803."

Notwithstanding the organization of Seneca County, in March, 1804, the County of Cayuga retained jurisdiction in this case, and Delaware John was tried at a court of Oyer and Terminer, held June 27, 1804, at the academy in the village of Aurora, by and before Honorable Ambrose Spencer, one of the judges of the Supreme Court Judicature, presiding, and upon his own confession of guilt, the murderer was adjudged guilty and sentenced to be hung, which sentence was carried into effect.

The County History of 1876, mentions the murder of a man in this county, committed by one Andrews, for which he was tried, convicted, sentenced and executed at Ovid, in the period, 1810 to 1812. Diligent inquiry to ascertain more definite data in relation to this case, failed to elicit additional information.

In later years, George Chapman, on July 20, 1828, murdered Daniel Wright in the town of Waterloo. He was tried and convicted at a term of court held at Waterloo, was sentenced and publicly hung there, May 28, 1829

The last execution for murder in this County was that of Charles Johnson, who, upon trial and conviction of the murder of John Walters, at the village of Waterloo, was sentenced and hung at the jail in that village, November 15 h, 1888.

There being two jails in this county the same are never crowded with prisoners. There has been no marked increase in the higher grades of crime, although with increase in population the number of convictions for minor offenses, punishable by sentence to jail, has increased, principally from vagrant tramps, as also the number of penitentiary cases.

In the palmy days of the local militia, this county had several militia regiments, and a number of independent military companies The military forces of the county, bore a prominent part in the War of 1812, and were also represented in the Mexican War In the Civil War (1861-1865(, the several towns were represented in the volunteer service and several residents of the County, arose to high rank in the military service. The County was also represented by a few volunteers, in the late war with

Spain.

There are now no military organizations in this County, and the days of "General Training" formerly so important an event, in early years, occur no more.

It is a matter for regret, that the "Town Meeting" occuring as an annual event in each town, every spring and which enabled our fathers to meet together and consider and perfect many measures thereat, for the local well-being, has in the past three years been consolidated with the general election and is now held biennially in the fall. Already, it is manifest, that town business has been greatly lost sight of, by this change, which has not been a beneficial one, and let us hope, for a return of the good old-fashioned Town Meeting, which was so greatly enjoyed in former years.

The History of Seneca County, edited by Hon. John Delafield, and published in 1850, and the County History published at Philadelphia in 1876, are indeed interesting and valuable publications, but the data thereof, should now be extended and brought down to the present time.

The history of the towns of Romulus and Varick, of the south towns, and of the town of Fayette, and the old town of Junius, (now comprising the four north towns) have also been partly written. Historical sketches of the villages of Waterloo and Seneca Falls have also been recently published. To complete the stories of the towns, that of the original military township of Ovid, now comprising the town of that name, with Covert and Lodi, remain to be written, and it rests with citizens of those towns, to undertake this good work.

Had time and space permitted, many other subjects might have been referred to, or considered at length, among which may be mentioned, the Pre-emption line; the Military Tract and Indian Reservations; the visit and reception of General La Fayette in this County, June 8, 1825; Negro Slavery in this County; early Town Meetings and elections; the Public Men of the County; The Woman's Rights Movement; roads, bridges and ferries; early births, marriages and deaths; early villages, cemeteries, taverns, stores and shops; early teachers and schools; and many other subjects, which must be left for the consideration of our Historical societies, and local historians in the several towns.

So too, no time is left for suitable mention and consideration of the vast progress made, in the century which the history of our County covers, the advancements made by the efforts and labors of the sturdy pioneer settlers, the great improvements produced by the power of steam and electricity; the developments made in manufactures, arts and sciences, and in short every department of life and business activity.

"A Century with all its hopes and fears,
Has sank into the deep abyss of time;
And on the threshold of the new, we stand,
Like travellers to a strange and distant clime."

During the century past, three average generations of men have passed away.

The transformation from 1804 to 1904, has been wrought with great labor and toil. Let us not forget the work of our fathers, now that we enjoy the comforts of life brought about by their exertions, with the advantages attained by education, religion, society, refinement and progress.

While we must not be unmindful of the past, let us enter upon the second century of our County, with the trust and confidence in the Divine Being, that He will direct the events of the future, as mercifully as He has done in the past.

I thank you for your kind attention, and will not forget my acknowledgements to several state and county officials and citizens, who assisted me, in collecting material presented for your consideration and in closing extend my very best wishes for the future of your Historical Society.

The Early Reformed Church.

By Rev. E. B. Van Arsdale.

At the very outset, I must acknowledge my indebtedness for all the facts this paper contains to others who have gone so thoroughly and carefully over the ground I am to cover as to make original research on my part absolutely unnecessary. Within the last decade, four churches in Seneca County have celebrated their centennials with public exercises, and ably qualified historians have gleaned from dusty records and local traditions, brought to light, and told in interesting form, the story of the early struggles and endeavors of the religious life of our county. I am only to repeat here, in as concise a manner as possible, what has already been told in other places.

I am restricted by the subject assigned me to the Early Reformed Church. I must confess that, when asked to present it, I was at a loss to understand why this particular denomination should have been selected for special attention upon this honorable occasion. It forms so small a part of the religious forces of the county. The three Dutch Reformed Churches situated at Lodi, Farmer and Tyre, and the German Reformed Church at Bearytown are all the Reformed churches in our bounds. However, historically considered, they are of interest and importance to us at this time.

Before I enter upon my special theme, I may be allowed some general notice of the early religious life of our county, since mine is the only paper that bears upon that subject. With the possible exception of traders with the Indians, the first white men to enter this immediate section before the American Revolution were Bishop John Frederic Christopher Cammerhoff and Rev. David Zeisberger, missionaries of the Moravian Church to the Indians. They made a tour from Wyoming,

Pennsylvania, in the summer of 1750, crossing from the eastern shore of Cayuga Lake, just above the present village of Union Springs, traversing the intervening forests to the outlet of Seneca Lake, and thence to the Genesee River, returning as they had come. Possibly, before their visit, Jesuit missionaries had ministered to the Indians between these lakes, as they did to the East, but no record of such service has been found. In 1765-66, Rev. Samuel Kirkland located for a time as a missionary to the Seneca Indians, a little distance west of the present city of Geneva, and in the course of his work, visited the eastern shores of Seneca Lake, where, on one occasion, he nearly lost his life at the hands of a hostile redskin. But these were all labors among the Aborigines, and, of course, have no bearing upon the development of the county.

Actual settlement by whites did not begin until the close of the Revolution. I suppose I ought to spare you the introduction of a name so familiar to you all. Job Smith, I suspect has been afflicted with a great deal of posthumous importance at the hands of your Historical Society, merely because he was venturesome enough to be the first settler in the county, here, at Seneca Falls, in 1787. He did not stay long. But his early departure in 1793 has not saved him from fame. The first permanent settlers who entered the county from the south by way of Sullivan's trail, were mostly adherents of the Reformed Churches of Pennsylvania and New Jersey. Many of them were veterans of that army whose march through the regions had revealed the rich fertility of its soil and the charming beauty of its landscape. They came with their families and belongings in great four-horse, canvas-topped wagons, cutting their way through dense forests, and building brush roads over the swamps. Later, there was an immigration into the north end of the county, largely from New England, by the water ways of the Mohawk, Oswego and Seneca River, and the lakes. At the beginning of the last decade of the eighteenth Century, there were probably not more than a dozen families between these lakes, scattered from the southwest corner of the present town of Lodi to Seneca Falls. For the most part, they were men who combined with their sturdiness and industry and independence, a firm faith in God and His Providence. They brought their religion with them into this virgin wilderness, and kept the light of faith burning upon the altars of their rude log cabins.

Between 1790 and 1800, the settlers came in much more rapidly, and missionaries from other regions were sent out to look after their spiritual interests, and to lay the foundations for church expansion. Gradually, the growing population was gathered into groups of worshippers, and churches began to be organized here and there, so that by the time of the formation of the present County of Seneca, in 1804, there were within its bounds five organized churches. Three of these were of the Presbyterian order, and two of them Baptist societies.

The first church organized in the county was the First Baptist of Romulus at Kendaia, constituted in June, 1795, with seven members. It was natural that this denomination should feel drawn at an early date to this well watered country. The Covert Baptist church was formed in February, 1803, with twenty eight members. The names of Jedediah Chapman and John Lindsley are prominent among the pioneer ministers of Western New York, the former located at Geneva and formed the Presbyterian church of that place in 1800. The latter organized a Presbyterian church within the bounds of the present town of Lodi, in the same year, which was the second church society in the county. He became its pastor and consequently was the first ordained clergyman to settle

in a regular charge in our county. Presbyterian churches were also established by Chapman at Romulus in April, 1802, and in the present village of Ovid, July, 1803. (He also founded the Presbyterian church of Seneca Falls in 1807.) These five were the church organizations already effected in the county at the time of its formal establishment—a constellation of religious centers for the fostering and promoting of the finest sentiments of our civilization in the early dawn of our history Itineraries of the Methodist Episcopal church also traversed this territory in those early days, preaching at Seneca Falls as early as 1797 at probably the first religious service held in that town. The Seneca Circuit grew out of this work, formed in 1804, and extending from the Clyde River to the Chemung with Seneca Falls as one of the appointments for regular visiting by the ministers. There seems, moreover, to have been a union organization effected by Chapman in the vicinity of Lodi village in 1803, composed partly of those disaffected from the Lindsley church.

This last organization is of interest to us because it erected the first house of worship in the county. It was constructed of hewn logs and stood upon a plot of ground given by Judge Silas Halsey, across the road from the grist mill he had built (also the first in the county) southwest from Lodi village, then known as DeMott's corners. This house was built just one hundred years ago so it was probably the only church building in the county at the time of its formation. The church founded by Rev. Lindsley likely erected a building soon after this, it may be in the same year. The early services of our fathers were held in homes, barns and schoolhouses, and sometimes in those great temples of nature, the vast aisled forests The appointments of worship were necessarily very crude. One has described the meeting in a barn, the congregation sitting upon upturned pails, boards and chunks of wood, some standing, the preacher upon a sleigh for a platform with an inverted box for a desk. And even in the churches there was little comfort, scarcely more than a shelter from the elements, the only heat from foot stoves, rough, high backed seats for the worshipper's comfort. Even the women attended church barefooted. But amid all the hardships and discomforts people attended upon the means of grace with zest and relish, walking long miles, perhaps driven partly, by a desire for neighborly interchange of news, but surely, too, by a high appreciation of the things of God—solace and stay for that rough life they lived. Sometimes these early places of worship were, to use the Irishman's phrase, "Filled to the brim inside and out"—and hundreds, unable to get room within, gathered around the church and listened to the preacher's voice coming through the open doors and windows.

We must now turn for a few moments to the special subject of our paper—The Early Reformed Church. A few words of explanation in regard to the Reformed Church will not be amiss. It is the term applied to that division of Protestantism that had its rise in Switzerland in 1516, under the leadership of Zwingli. It was contemporary with but distinct from the Lutheran movement. It soon gained a foothold in the German centers of Switzerland and in the Palatinate, in Holland and in France. The Reformed church in America is the descendant of the Reformation in Holland. The Reformed Church in the United States, to which the church at Bearytown belongs, is descended from the German church. The Reformed type of Christian doctrine is Calvinistic, as taught by the Heidelberg catechism, in close agreement with the Westminister confession of the Presbyterian church to which it is closely allied, also in form of government—the form which is most in accord with our Republican institutions. Indeed, later scholars contend that Holland more than any other country has furnished the principles upon which our natural institutions are founded.

The Protestant faith was held in Holland at the greatest sacrifice. They long defied Philip II. and his minions backed as they were, by the whole military and ecclesiastical resources of Spain, then the greatest power in the world. So calamitous was its condition during the eighty years war that the Reformed Church called itself "The Church under the Cross." Finally, its indomitable pluck and persistence wore out the spirit of its foe. It then became the asylum of all the persecuted of other lands. The Pilgrims from England sought refuge there before braving the dangers of the sea and the perils of the inhospitable shores of New England. The Huguenots, driven from France, found safety and liberty in Holland and identified themselves with the Dutch Reformed church.

Our great commonwealth of New York is closely related to this brave people, as they were its first colonists. In 1609, Hendrick Hudson, in the employ of the Dutch West India Company, entered New York bay and sailed up the North River. In 1614 a trading post was established on Manhattan Island and our great metropolis was born. In 1623 a permanent agricultural settlement was made and in 1628 a church was organized which has had a continuous existence to this day and is with reason supposed to be the oldest Protestant church on this continent. Other churches of Hollanders and Huguenots were established along the Hudson and Mohawk and in New Jersey and Pennsylvania. The German branch of the Reformed church entered later and was built up principally in Pennsylvania. Now this country was settled largely by the children of this German, Huguenot and Dutch ancestry, coming from New Jersey and Pennsylvania. They are staunch adherents of the faith of their fathers. We have referred to the church founded by Rev. John Lindsley in 1800. It was organized as the First Presbyterian Church of Ovid, and was the first society in the town of Ovid, then comprising also the towns of Lodi and Covert. A large element in its membership were of Reformed lineage. And it was not strange that, in 1809, after four years of occasional missionary ministrations during the vacancy of the pulpit, its affiliation was transferred to the classes of Montgomery of the Reformed Church and the Rev. Abraham Brokaw became its settled pastor. Under his guidance it prospered greatly and its membership grew to over two hundred.

Everything went well until 1822, when the church was rent by that secession movement from the Reformed Church that resulted in the forming of the True Reformed Church. The pastor, a majority of the officers and but a minority of the congregation joined the secession. Litigation over the property followed until the value of it was eaten up by legal costs. But the title was awarded to that larger part of the congregation that held to the old consecrated name and relations.

Being in need of a church home, it was decided to build in the village of Lodi, upon the site where the present edifice stands. It was at this time that the congregation of the old log church, of which we have spoken, aided in the erection of a new house of worship and shared its privileges. It was afterwards merged into the Lodi Reformed Church.

It was about this time, also, that the pastor of the Lodi church began to fill a regular appointment at Farmerville. The old church had been situated on the road, one mile north of the highway between Lodi and Farmer, and about halfway between the two localities, so that the inhabitants of the vicinity naturally drawn to that church could readily attend. After the removal to Lodi, it became necessary for the preacher to bring his message to them in their own village. This eventually resulted in the organization of another Reformed Church in Farmer, in November 1830, which, with the Baptist Church of the same village, organized ten years earlier from the mother church at Covert has been the center of christian influence and power for good in that community.

The church that was organized as the True Dutch Church by those who seceded from the old mother church in 1822 erected a house of worship about o e-half mile east of the old edifice. Dominie Brokaw continued his ministry there until 1838, when he was succeeded by Rev. Archibald McNiel until 1865. he was the last pastor, and the church he had served so long and faithfully became known locally as the McNiel Church. The society finally disbanded, and the building was taken down about 1876. Nothing now remains to mark the site of either of these two old churches except the little grave yard in the vicinity which is now seldom used.

It may be well to insert a few items of historical interested closely connected with the life of this early Reformed Church of the old town of Ovid, in the present town of Lodi. The first settler in what is now the town of Lodi was George Fausett, who located directly upon Sullivan's trail. He became a member of this church, and his daughter was the first child born in the town, probably in the county. Silas Halsey, another early arrival in this section, and staunch friend and supporter of this church built the first grist mill in the county, gave the plot of ground for the first church edifice and for a cemetery, and served as the first county clerk. The first public religious services known to have been held in this county were held in 1794 at the house of Abraham Covert, in the town of Ovid. He was a Jerseyman and a faithful son of the Reformed Church.

There is an interesting incident related in connection with the marriage of his son. "It was the first marriage which took place in the town. It occurred in 1795, was a triple marriage. The parties were Abraham A. Covert and Catherine Covert, Joseph Wilson and Anna Wyckoff, Enoch Covert and Jane Stewart They were obliged to cross Seneca Lake to find a justice authorized to perform the ceremony."

A little later than their Dutch cousins from New Jersey settled in Ovid, Germans from Pennsylvania, with a few from the fatherland, began making homes for themselves in the town of Fayette. They brought with them the same love for the Reformed faith of their fathers and their same respect for education, and early built the church and school. The first clergyman to settle in the town of Fayette was the Rev. Anthony Houtz of the German Reformed Church, who took up his residence there just one hundred years ago, 1804. Before his coming, this community, with others in the county, had enjoyed occasional preaching services in school buildings, barns and private houses. For several years after his coming he served the people in the capacity of pastor, preaching in the German language, in the Burgh school house and at the residence of Henry Singer at Bearytown. Finally, on December 26, 1809, the first attempt at formal church organization was made at a meeting of German Reformed and Lutheran residents at the Burgh school house. This is the origin of the oldest existing church organization in the town of Fayette. Steps were soon taken to provide for a suitable house of worship to be used by both denominations, and probably early in 1813 the building was dedicated. It was a log structure 22 by 28 feet, built upon the site of the present stone edifice of the Christ Reformed Congregation at Bearytown. Rev. Houtz had a preaching station also at West Fayette, from which Jerusalem Church was formed in the summer of 1811. (It appears also from denominational records that the town of Fayette was visited for a period of years, 1817 to 1825, by missionaries sent out by the Dutch Reformed Church, but no permanent church organization resulted from their labors.) No sketch of this Reformed Church in Fayette would be complete without allusion to one of its pastorates, remarkable as the longest in the annals of the county and seldom surpassed in the record of any church I refer to the ministry of Rev. Diedrich Willers, D. D., who for a period of nearly sixty-one years, from 1821 to 1882, served this church. His work was largely that of a pioneer pastor. Beside his duties to his own people he served also at different times at six

other places in the county and at seven or eight other points in Tompkins, Cayuga, Wayne, Livingston and Niagara counties, performing a large portion of the travel, incident to so extended a field of labor, on horseback, in the early years of his ministry. The power of the church in any community is largely commensurate with the personal force of its representatives, that is, its members, above all its ministry. The influence of one such sturdy, indefatigable, devout leader in a community for so long a period is simply inestimable and far surpasses, in the depth of the impression it makes, the strongest influence of shorter pastorates however brilliant or impressive. The impress of that one character, noble and faithful, identified so closely with all that the church stands for, so conspicuously before the eyes of men, puts a stamp upon the life within its radius that endures for generations. And the church that furnishes such a center of religious life is an estimable factor in the development of a town's life and gives it strong claims upon the respect and gratitude of the people.

The only other Reformed Church in the county besides these three I have mentioned, is that at Tyre, which was organized in 1835, as the result of a union with a Presbyterian Church formed in the vicinity a few years before. The date of its formation is too late to include it among the early churches to which my paper is limited.

This resume of the churches of this order reveals the fact that, although they have not become numerous within our territory, they have been influential in the life of the county from the beginning of its history, intimately associated as they were with the first things of its life, but also of our state and county.

In the time allotted for this paper, it has been impossible to do more than touch upon the beginning of the church life of our county, although one is strongly tempted to go more into detail, and digress into paths that would lead us among the daily surroundings of our fathers, and to show them in their hardships and their triumphs

23

which their sturdy religious faith sinewed them to bear. It is only by a few flashes of light upon the screen that I have attempted to help you enter by imagination into their early struggles. These men and women of indefatigable labor, undaunted courage, and undoubting faith, laid the foundation of our present luxurious and comfortable living, of our hopeful outlook on the future, and of our trusting uplook and upreach for things of the spirit that make for righteousness, love and peace. As the spirit of the English Puritan, and the Scotch Covenanter, and the French Huguenot, and the sturdy Dutchman, and his phlegmatic German brother lived in the early settlers of this county, prompt-

ing them to bring their faith and zeal to this virgin wilderness of forest and morass as their fathers had brought them to these untried shores, so may it abide in us, the source of that intelligent and virtuous manhood which must ever be the bed rock of permanency for our American institutions. Hand in hand with the school that promotes the intelligence which a free people always need for self-government, and with the court which maintains and administers laws of equity and justice, must go the church which fosters that regard for virtue and right, and that faith that purifies and ennobles the life which uses the unexcelled priveleges our civilization puts into our hands.

Preservation of Private and Public Records.

By Dr. William Austin Macy.

We must assume that the preservation of private and public records is of importance to the individual and to the state. If we do not, then what have we for the historian to base his account of the times in which we live, and too, without a history, is not a people without the incentive to right living and thinking in many ways. If we live without recording what will point out the differences between us and those who have gone before or those who come after, are we not then living to a great extent as the trees live, and who shall tell the tale when time rolls around.

From the earliest times we have yet to look for a people who did not in some way seek to preserve their own histories, not only tribal but the personal histories of the families which made up the aggregation of people. For only do we find by tradition and written history that private and public histories of men and their times have been handed down, but all along the way, as far back as we can go, we find examples of the greatest and best of people encouraging us to keep our histories, and in modern times the greatest of our citizens have encouraged those around them to emulate the past and do better in this respect.

In a country where the elementary population has changed to the extent that ours has, and where even greater changes are likely to take place in the future, it would seem that if we would have the posterity of a few generations know anything at all about their forbears more attention than has often excited would have to used, or they would be a nameless race among those who would have a history.

Possibly the best use for the preservation of family history or genealogy, is to serve to stimulate those who come after to right living and to vie with those who have gone before in living so that clean records and lives of much usefulness to their fellowmen, may be the records that will be written. Let a man have ever so much of this world's goods and yet how much of it can be really used for his actual necessities? If our American people are always too interested in the making of money only, what of the responsibilities of the use of what is left behind by those who have acquired?

What have we to say of the rational incentive to get ahead in the world in the average individual? No matter how ambitious the individual may be, together with whatever he does or succeeds to, runs the responsibility of the individual in the many other directions of life. If he shakes them off he is only one-sided and he lives the most selfish and sordid life. He lives only to himself, losing in this the very best that would otherwise come to him. That we make comparisons then, a history is necessary, and it is of use to preserve for the future a record of kinship and ancestry, that it may be helpful in these ways and many more which I will not take the time to point out now.

When we stop to ascertain what has been done in preserving private and public records we are at once struck with the fact that to-day there is ten times and more the interest in these matters than there was only a few years ago. That this is due in large part to the formation of our various patriotic and colonial societies is probably true, but this has been helpful in two ways. It has stimulated actual patriotism and helped to make our men and women better citizens because they have had a greater pride in their country. It has also caused them to study in more detail what has helped to make the greatness of this our country and to glory more than they ever thought of doing in the good deeds of their ancestors. All this has immediately required that if they knew who their forbears were, that their records should be preserved and those of us who have taken interest in these matters from a love of history, etc., have watched with much pleasure this growth of interest in these directions.

The tendency formerly was to give too little care to any records or documents when they were once through with for the time being, and we find in making our inquiries into these matters that any kind of a place is usually provided for all kinds of public and private records until the public conscience is awakened and they learn how easily these things disappear and are lost to the future. Often have we found and are to find that even in the case of county and other very important records including court records, that at such a time all were burnt up, find the collection of years consumed in smoke. I remember reading a letter from a correspondent in the Island of Jamaica, that at a certain time when their Island was under martial law, the Governor ordered many loads of the rarest papers relating to the Island's history to be turned into the Rio Cobre, one of their principal rivers, with the words, "Away with the accursed past." Yet the memory of the past is one of those things which encourages us most to trust to the consolations of religion and live so that the review at the end of life will be to our credit rather than the reverse.

Little by little we are gathering up and caring for our historic relics. All over the country historical societies are doing good work and we are only doing in this country that which is being done the world over. In Massachusetts, an enabling act has been had which assists them in gradually getting the vital statistics of all their towns placed in print and preserved, and these are being issued to such subscribers, including public libraries, etc. at the nominal sum of a cent a page, including binding. A move is being made to get the other New England States to do the same thing and it is to be hoped that all of our own early records will one day be placed in print, so that those studying the early colonial history, will have less difficulty in getting actual facts on which to build.

In the matter of collecting family history the society to do the most and best work is the New York Genealogical and Biographical Society, of New York State. This society has its headquarters at New York City, where it has its own fire-proof building and fire-proof vaults, and it has supplemented the work done by the New York Historical Society and the other historical societies of the state by collecting as much of strictly family history as has been possible. I have had the honor for a few years past to represent this Society in Seneca County as a member of their Research Committee, and it was one of the purposes of my attendance at your anniversary meeting to say to your members how much our society is interested in all historical work, particularly in the preservation of family histories, and how glad they would be through myself to receive such historical notes of any of the families of this district as might be prepared and submitted for preservation. I have had some very interesting notes given me of this kind and I am promised more and I would at all times be glad to act in bringing any work of this kind before our Society and in seeing that it is preserved for the future use of the many others who would thus acquire a larger opportunity for consulting what they would naturally look to such a repository of such information and expect to find more easily, as it accumulates, than in the hands of private individuals where it is more likely to be lost or destroyed. I would then ask that those who would desire to save family genealogies as may have been compiled, family bible records which in time disappear, and other historical information which is worthy of being perpetuated, should send me neatly made copies for the purpose of their being deposited with the central society and will assist in any way possible such as are desirous of starting information, if they will be good enou_h in writing to enclose return postage that the burden may not be too much one way.

In listening to the many interesting particulars of the Hon. Mr. Willers' most interesting paper, and in considering the work you are attempting to do in Seneca County, I am struck with the fact that there does not seem to be any very general move to collect from all sources systematically, but only from your one town. Considering that you have a sister society in Waterloo, I think it is a pity that a move cannot be made to form a general county society, whose membership should extend to all who might be interested in your work, including the descendants of former residents of Seneca County Such societies do a much larger work, and by charging a nominal fee which all would feel they could afford, it is possible to collect from so large a number if any proper interest is developed, that a good publication fund can be established and something really well gotten up can be presented each year to the members, and disbursed at an increase in price to such others as may show interest and want

copies of the Collections of the Society. A number of such societies are under way and doing excellent work and many more will undoubtedly be formed as time progresses.

Why not test the public interest in a suggestion of this kind and see whether chapters of a few active workers can not be established in each town, who can work with the officers of the central society in collecting systematically what would be placed in print at the end of each year? I am of the opinion that a movement of this kind would awaken considerable interest and I know personally of one or more collections already, of matters of much interest, which would probably be contributions towards establishing a collection in which Seneca County would feel a special pride. Personally I would prefer to see any collection of relics of historic value given to the largest public library which might become established in the county, provided always that this was a fire proof building with other facilities for storing Mss given to it, etc.

I have suggested that this matter be opened to discussion in the papers of the county, and if sufficient interest to justify us is manifested, that some of us get together and see what can be done in really establishing a movement that shall react to the credit and renown of Seneca County.

Judiciary of the Connty of Seneca.

BY HON. JOHN E. RICHARDSON.

On the 20th day of April 1777, the representatives of the State of New York assembled at Kingston and adopted the first Constitution of the State of New York. Under that constitution the County Judge or the first Judge of the County of Seneca were appointed officers. The 23rd sub-division of said Constitution provides that all officers other than those who by this constitution are directed to be otherwise appointed, shall be appointed in the manner following, to wit : The Assembly shall once in each year, openly nominate and appoint one of the Senators from each great district, which Senator will form a council for the appointment of the said officers, and which the Governor for the time being shall be president and have a casting vote, but no other vote ; and with the advice and consent of said Council shall appoint all the said officers.

That the first Judge of the County Court in every County shall hold office during good behavior or until they shall have attained the age of sixty years. This provision continued in force until 1822 when said consti itution was amended empowering the Governor with the consent of the Senate to make such judicial appointments and such appointive power continued until said constitution was amended by Chapter 276 of the laws of 1847, which provides for the election on the 8th day of June following of a County Judge who shall enter upon the duties of his office July 1st following his election and hold office for the term of four years from the 1st day of January next ; and, after the expiration of the term of office of those first elected the term of office of said officer shall be four years.

By virtue of the power conferred upon said Council of Appointment Cornelius Humphrey was the first judge appointed in and for the County of Seneca and the following is a copy of the certificate showing his appointment :—for which I am indebted to Hon. J. B. H. Mougin, Deputy Secretary of State.

"At a meeting of the Council of Appointment held at the Chambers of His Excellency the Governor, in the City of Albany on Monday, the 2nd day of April, 1804.

Present, his Excellency George Clinton, Esquire, President.

The Honorable John Broome, Caleb Hyde, Thomas Tredwell, Esqrs. Members.

Resolved, that a general commission issue for the County of Seneca, that the following persons be and they are hereby appointed Civil Officers of said county, viz.

Cornelius Humphrey, Grover Smith, John Sayre, Judges and Justices of the Peace.

Jonas Whiting of Ulysses, James Van Horn of Ovid, Asa Smith of Romulus, Benajah Boardman of Washington, assistant justices and justices.

Justices of the Peace, James Jackson, Stephen Woodworth, John Townsend, Jr , Ovid ; Thomas Shepardson, Ulysses ; Daniel Everts, Hector ; John Hood, Washington ; Lewis Birdsall, Jesse Southwick, Junius.

Jared Sanford, Surrogate ; Silas Halsey, County Clerk ; William Smith, Sheriff ; Charles Thompson, Coroner.

Geo. Clinton,
Jno. Broome
Caleb Hyde,
Thomas Tredwell.

Judge Humphrey served with honor and distinction until May, 1809, as is shown by the records of the Court of this County. He was born in 1735 ; he served as colonel in the Revolutionary war and was a member of the

Second Provincial Congress and as a Representative from Dutchess County in the Senate and Assembly. He came to Seneca County about the year 1801 and located in what is now known as the town of Ulysses and represented this county in the Assembly 1806-07.

The first court in the County of Seneca was held in the house of John Seeley on lot No. 3 in the town of Ovid, and held there almost continuously until May, 1807, at which time court was adjourned to the first Tuesday in October to the Court House in the town of Ovid, but when court convened the Court House was not comple'ed and the court was adjourned to the house of John Seeley and continued to adjourn from time to time to the house of John Seeley until the second Tuesday of May, 1808, when the first court was held in the Court House in the village of Ovid. The judges holding said court were Cornelius Humphrey, first judge, Grover Smith, John Sayre and Benjamin Pelton.

The first court held in Waterloo was a Term of the General sessions of the Peace, May 12, 1818, and was presided over by Justices John Sayre, John Burton and Benjamin Hendricks and were so held until March 29, 1822, when an act was passed by the Legislature which provided,

"That the several courts of the common pleas, general sessions of the pence, circuit courts and oyer and terminer, hereafter to be holden in and for the County of Seneca, shall be held alternately at the court house in the town of Ovid, and at the court house in the town of Junius; and that the next May term of the court of common pleas and general sessions of the peace, in and for said county, shall be held at the court house in the town of Ovid; and all writs and process whatsoever, returnable in said courts, at the next day May term thereof, shall be taken and deemed returnable at the said court house in the town of Ovid; and all persons who are or shall be bound or required to appear at the said next May term of the said courts, or either of them, by bond, recog. nizance, or otherwise shall be taken,

deemed and considered, to be bound and required to appear at the court house in the town of Ovid, aforesaid, and the first circuit court and oyer and terminer, to be held for the said county shall be held at the court house in the town of Junius."

"That from and after the passage of this act, there shall be two jury districts in the county of Seneca, the first to comprise the towns of Covert, Ovid and Romulus, and the second the towns of Fayette, Junius, Galen and Wolcott; and the clerk of said county shall keep the names of the Jurors in such districts separate, and the jurors shall be drawn for each court, from the jury district in which the court is to be held."

"That it shall not be lawful for the supervisors of the said county to sell the court house in the town of Ovid, or the lot of land on which the same stands, any law heretofore made to the contrary notwithstanding."

The county court until the adoption or the Constitution in 1846 was divided into two branches, one known as the Court of Common Pleas which had jurisdiction of Civil Matters and a Criminal Court called General Sessions of the Peace; the other court to which we have the honor of referring to is the Surrogate's Court.

May 31st 1809, Benjamin Pelton was appointed first judge and served until 1812. He came to the town of Ulysses about 1802. He served as a captain of the Revolutionary War and died in Ithaca about 1830.

Oliver C. Comstock was appointed first judge May, 1812, and served until April 13, 1815. Judge Comstock was a man representing three professions, a doctor, lawyer and minister. He served Seneca county as Member of Assembly and as a representative in Congress afterwards served as Chaplain of Congress. Judge Comstock was born in Warwick, Kent County, Rhode Island. He died at the home of his son in Marshall, Calhoun County, Michigan January 11, 1860.

Judge Comstock was succeeded April 13, 1815, by John Knox who served until June 18, 1818. Judge Knox died August 1, 1853, aged about seventy years. He was a man of much learning and it has been said of him that his success was largely due to his magnetic personality and judgment displayed in his business Common sense was his motto in conducting cases rather than common law, and he like most of the early practitioners took great delight in aiding a young man rather than discouraging him.

On June 18, 1818, John McLean, Jr., was appointed to said position and served until January 30, 1823.

Luther Stevens succeeded John McLean, Jr., January 30, 1823, and served until March 13, 1833.

March 13, 1833, Jesse Clarke was appointed to that honored position and served until July 1, 1817. Judge Clark was born in Berkshire County, Mass., where he acquired, chiefly through his own efforts as a teacher, a liberal education. He came to Waterloo in 1814, and commenced the practice of law, and soon, by his superior talents and education rose to an enviable prominence and success in his profession. At the election under the Constitution of 1821 he was chosen one of the senators for the western district He died May 20, 1849.

In July 1847, the term of James K. Richardson, the first elective county judge of the county of Seneca commenced. He served until January 1, 1852. Judge Richardson was born at West Burlington, Otsego county, in this state, October 3, 1806, and died at Waterloo, October 9, 1875. Being my father I thought I would much rather spread upon this paper the thoughts of the members of the Bar of the County of Seneca rather than my own estimate of the man, but to my utter astonishment I find that the records of the proceeding of the courts of this county, from the time my father was elected to the present, contained memorial articles relating to every judge who has departed this life except James K Richardson. I find in an issue of the Waterloo Observer the week that my father died that the members of the bar assembled at the office of Judge Hadley and they then chose Judge Hadley, William H. Bur-

ton Esq., and Charles A. Hawley, Esq., a committee to draft and present resolutions to the next term of court I cannot believe that the committee failed to do their duty as I believe Judge Richardson was honored and respected by all, and the only excuse I can find is that the county clerk was too tired at that time to record the proceedings of the committee and the court in adopting their kind words. I do find in the edition of the Waterloo Observer above referred to, the following:

"Judge James K. Richardson was born in Otsego county, in 1806. In obedience to the wishes of his father, who was a physician of note in that county, he studied medicine, but on the very day that he attained the age of of twenty-one years, he relinquished all idea of following that profession which was distasteful to him, came to Waterloo and commenced reading law in the office of Messrs. Samuel Clark and Daniel Ruggles. Shortly after he was called to the bar, he left for the west, but returned to New York State in a year or two afterwards, opening an office at Sodus, Wayne county, and continued practicing law in that county for five years. Mr. Samuel Clarke, the same under whom he had studied law, then offered him a partnership in his business in Waterloo which the deceased accepted, and he has ever since resided here. In politics Mr. Richardson was always a very strong Republican, and for many years he contributed very largely to the Seneca Falls Courier, a fact not generally known. He was elected county judge at the first election under the new constitution of 1876, and in the twofold capacity of judge and surrogate he earned for himself a true record of honesty and uprightness, and here we may use the expression made to us yesterday by one of the oldest of the bar in Seneca County, 'that he was an honest and upright man as ever lived, professionally or otherwise." He made a most excellent surrogate, always careful and accommodating, he was perfectly competent and was remarkable for the methodical way in which his papers were always kept."

Judge Richardson was succeeded by
John E Seeley who served from Jan-
uary 1, 1852 to January 1856. Judge
Seeley died March 30, 1875. He received his acidemical education at the
Ovid Academy, under the tuition of
William rvin, after which he passed
through a full course of study at Yale
College, where he graduated in 1835.
He then studied law in this village at
the office of Hon John Maynard
About the year 1836 or '37 he located
at Monroe, Michigan, but returned to
Ovid in 1839. In the campaign of
1840, he was a very active Harrison
man—was chairman of the town committee. In 1842, he was supervisor of
the town In 1848, he acted with the
"Free Soil" party, and in 1857 was
elected Judge of the county by the
united vote of the Democratic and
Free Soil Party, running ninety-seven
votes ahead of his ticket in this town,
He represented this district in the first
Republican National Convention, and
was the presidential elector for this
district in 1860, and again in 1864 and
elected to Congress in 1870; was a
trustee of Willard Asylum and I think
president of the board from its organization, until after he was elected to
Congress, when he resigned. In every
station of life he was always to be
trusted. In all public enterprise he
took an active part, and when money
was to be raised, he was generally at
the head of the list. He was an un-
comprising foe to slavery; the black
man had no truer friend.

Sterling G. Hadley succeeded Judge
Seeley and served until 1860. Judge
Hadley was born in the town of Goshen,
Litchfield County, Conn, August 26,
1812, and died at Waterloo, September
1, 1901. His early years were passed
in different places where the family resided, and he fitted for college at Egre-
mont Academy. In 1833 he entered
Union College at Schenectady, N. Y.,
from which he graduated in 1836, and
afterward he taught in the Avon
Springs Academy. April 1, 1837, he
came to Waterloo, where he since resided. He read law with Hon Samuel
Birdsall and was admitted to the bar

in 1839, after which he was in partnership with his former preceptor for four
years. Later, forming a partnership
with John McAllister, he continued
with that gentlemen under the firm
title of McAllister & Hadley, until the
death of the former. For ten years
he was Justice of the Peace, but resigned upon his election as County
Judge and Surrogate for a term of
four years. Nor did his public service
end here. On the Democratic ticket
he was elected a member of the Lower
House of the Legislature. The Governor tendered him the appointment of
State Assessor, which position he held
for several years, and which took him
into every county of the state. He
was also president of the Board of
Managers of the State Hospital located
on Seneca lake.

In 1859 George Franklin was elected
county judge; he was re-elected in
1867 and again in 1877 and served
fourteen years. Judge Franklin was
born in the town of Hector, December
8. 1819 and died in the village of Ovid
April 24, 1886. He was an upright,
conscientious man, a father and friend
to the young practitioner, more than
willing to aid him in his work and we
do not think that the worth of Judge
Franklin and the loss that was sustained in his death can be any better
expressed than was done by Hon. Gilbert Wilcoxen, Frederick L. Manning,
Charles A. Hawley, William C. Hazelton and John E Richardson, a committee appointed April 28, 1886 by
the Seneca County Bar to express their
thoughts on the occasion of the death
of Judge Franklin which reads as
follows:

"In the death of Hon. George
Franklin the bar has sustained no
common loss. Three times elected
Judge and Surrogate of Seneca County
he discharged the important duties of
the office with rare fidelity and ability.
He possessed and deserved the confidence of the bar and the people for
he was a judge without fear and without reproach. He had an eminently
logical and judicial mind and his de-
cisions were almost uniformly sound
and correct. He was not technical but

31

based his judicial action upon broad and equitable principles.

As a lawyer he won the admiration and regard of his brethren and of his clients as well.

He was a man of wide and varied attainments. The classics were the delights of his leisure hours; and he was intimately acquainted with what is best and brightest in English literature.

But we who have known him so long and so well delight to remember him not only as the just and upright judge and the able and honest lawyer but to recall the charm of his manner, the warmth of his heart and his unusual accomplishments in social life. We shall cherish the memory of his genial presence and in all the years to come shall feel our loss.

We tender to his family and to the community where he was best known and loved and honored our sympathy in his hour of sorrow."

Gilbert Wilcoxen.
Frederick L. Manning
Charles A. Hawley
William C. Hazelton
John E Richardson,
Committee.

Seneca County Court May 25, 1889.

Presented and read in open court and motion ordered entered upon the minvtes of the court, and so entered.

Abram Wilson, Dep. Clerk.

In 1863 Josiah T. Miller was elected and entered upon the duties of the office and served the people until January 1, 1868. Judge Josiah T. Miller was born in April 1820 in Parry Co., Pa.; he came to Seneca County at an early age and in 1850 and 1859 served the county as District Attorney; in 1860 he was appointed on the staff of Governor Seymour and in 1869 he represented the county in the Assembly; and my feeble words can not express the loss to the Bar of the County of Seneca in the death of Judge Miller as do the proceedings of the committee appointed to do honor to his memory and for that reason I give in full the proceedings of the County Court as shown by the record.

"In re the death
of
Hon. Josiah T. Miller

In honor to the memory of Josiah T. Miller deceased, the following resolutions were introduced by Jasper N. Hammond, Attorney at Law, Seneca Falls, N. Y.,

WHEREAS, The Bar of Seneca County are grieved to learn of the death of Hon. Josiah Thompson Miller, at his residence in Waterloo in the early morning of Tuesday the 25th instant, and

WHEREAS, We deem it fitting that we should in a public manner record our deep sorrow for the death of a man who for so many years has been a leader of this bar and has had justly conferred upon him so many of its honors. We his brethren in the profession of the law have therefore,

Resolved, That we bow with reverence and resignation to the decree of Providence that has deprived us of a personal and professional friend, and in common with the community at large mourn his loss, we recognize Judge Miller's distinguished professional ability and profound and thorough learning in the law.

To the discharge of the duties of his profession he brought a high sense of professional honor, and a wealth of legal learning and resource. Guided by a strong sense of justice, he was fearless in the maintainance of matured opinion. As a judge he was able and upright, ever tempering justice with mercy. He won the respect of the Bench and Bar and with all with whom he associated. And it is further

Resolved, That while we are proud of these professional attainments and honors of our departed friend which in a large sum are public property we gratefully record these private personal attributes which made so very pleasant our intercourse with him. A genial and courteous gentleman he treated with consideration the opinion and respected the qualities of his equals in position at the Bar and to its younger members he was a constant and valued friend ever ready to help by wise counsel, and direct them with the treasures of his large experience.

To the lowly he was a constant bene-
factor and no poor man's cause with
justice in it was ever declined by him.
And it is further

Resolved, That to his stricken family
we tender our sincerest sympathy in
their great bereavement.

Resolved, That this Bar attend the
funeral of our friend in a body and
that these resolutions be presented at
the next term of the Supreme Court in
this county, and to the next term of
the Seneca County Court, and be published in the county Press and a copy
of the same suitably engrossed be presented to the family of the deceased.

William H. Burton
Jasper N. Hammond
John Landon Kendig
Com. of Sen. Co. Bar.

These resolutions were adopted by
and spread upon the minutes of the
court November 11, 1884.

Gilbert Wilcoxen was elected county
judge in 1871 and served for six years
and is one of the two ex county judges
who is permitted to be with us to day.
Judge Wilcoxen was born in the town of
Smithfield, Madison Co., N. Y., Septem-
ter 25, 1828 He moved to Seneca
Falls in 1839 and graduated from
Hamilton College in 1852. On leaving college he selected the legal profession and immediately entered the
office of the late Judge Miller at Seneca Falls, and was admitted to practice
in 1854 but did not commence the
practice of his profession until 1860;
as an attorney and counselor he has
won great distinction for his learning
and ability; and contrary to the usual
avocation of an attorney he has been
president of the Seneca Falls Savings
Bank for more than twenty years.
Prior to his election as county judge
he represented his town, Seneca Falls,
in the Board of Supervisors.

In 1883 Peter H. Van Auken was
elected county judge and served six
years and is the second ex-judge living.
Judge Van Auken was born in Guilder-
land, Albany County, N. Y. He was
admitted to the bar at Troy, in 1859,
from thence he went to Phelps, Ontario county, and opened an office.

He took up his residence at Seneca
Falls in 1861 and from 1862 to 1864
was in business with the late Judge
Miller. Being a very learned man his
ability was appreciated by the electors
from the fact that before being elected
to the office of county judge, he was
honored by his town in having been
chosen Supervisor, Member of the
Board of Education and Justice of the
Peace and his departure to Rochester,
his present home, was regretted by all
who knew him.

William C. Hazelton was elected
county judge in 1889 and served until
January 1, 1896. Judge Hazelton was
born in Tompkins county, September
1, 1835 and died on the town of Ovid,
in this county March 2. 1898. He
followed the life of a farmer until
about 1855 when he entered the office
of Dana, Beers & Howard of Ithaca
and was admitted to the bar in 1858.
In 1862 he was elected district attorney
of the county and served three years.
In 1868 he was re-elected and served a
third term in 1880 In 1873 he was
elected member of assembly. He was
a good lawyer, ever striving to make
the facts of any matter submitted to
him correspond with the law in the
matter so that if he brought an action
he would have the law and facts both
on his side.

In November 1895 John E. Richardson was elected to succeed Judge Hazelton and served for six years. And in
November 1901 the electors, contrary
to custom, re-elected him to succeed
himself.

John E. Richardson was born September 10. 1846 in the village of Waterloo
in this county and attended the common
school; in 1866 he entered the office of
the late Judge Hadley and there gained
the rudiments of his legal education.
From Judge Hadley's office he went
to the Albany Law School graduating
there in 1868 since which time he has
been practicing in the village of his
birth.

In the early days of the Court of
Common Pleas and the Court of Sessions there were associated with the
first judge, justices of the peace who
were at times called judges and among

those were Garry V. Sackett, Grover Smith, John Sayre, William Molton, James Van Horn, Jared Sandford, Robert Swarthout,Tomkins C Delevan, John Sutton, Jacob L. Larzelere, Thomas White, John Maynard, David Burroughs, Thomas C. Magee, Abraham Sebring, John Burton and Benjamin Headricks.

The only other court which would come under the subject of the Judiciary of the County of Seneca is the Surrogate's Court.

The first Surrogate appointed was Jared Sandford and the first court held was in the town of Ovid, and the first will admitted to probate was that of Issac Hagerman of Ovid, June 7, 1804. And the first letters of administration were issued June 10, 1804, on the estate of David Kelly, late of the town of Ovid, N. Y. Jared Sandford was appointed April 2, 1804 and served until April 14, 1811, he was re-appointed April 6th, 1813 and served until February 28, 1815

John Sayre was appointed surrogate February 14, 1811 and served until 1813. Judge Sayre was born in the town of Booming Grove, Orange Co. N. Y., July 24, 1767; he died March 4, 1848; September 2. 1800 he was chosen Supervisor of Romulus and re elected year after year until 1808; he was re-elected supervisor in 1830 31 32. In 1804 he was elected the first member of assembly and re-elected in 1808 and again in 1831; he served as treasurer of the county from 1817 to 1821. For many years he was associate judge of the Seneca County Courts and was the first postmaster of Romulus.

William Thompson was chosen surrogate February 28, 1815 and served until April 3, 1819, he was re-appointed March 31, 1821 and served until December 3, 1827.

Judge Thompson was born in Stillwater, Saratoga Co. N. Y., March 4, 1785, he graduated at Union College, Schenectady, N. Y., in 1806. After completing his college studies he entered the office of his brother James who was practicing law in Milton, Saratoga Co., N. Y. In the spring of 1812 he found his new home and

pitched his tent in the town of Ovid in this county. It is said of him "Not greedy of gain, he did not use his influence as a lawyer in the promotion of strife, but often counciled amicable sett'ement of difficulties between contending parties." Though not seeking preferment, he was more than once called to represent his county in the Legislative Halls of the state, and by his acknowledged ability and popularity succeeded to the Speaker's chair. He died November 18, 1871.

Luther F. Stevens was appointed surrogate April 3, 1819 and served as such until March 31, 1821.

December 3, 1827. Samuel Birdsall was appointed surrogate. Judge Birdsall was born May 14, 1791 at Hillsdale, Columbia Co, N. Y. In the year 1817 he moved to Waterloo and for more than half a century after settling in Waterloo his position was one of prominence and influence and among the many honorable positions filled by him were Master in Chancery; Division Judge Advocate; with the rank of Colonel; Counsellor in the Supreme Court; Surrogate of Seneca County; District Attorney of the county; postmaster at Waterloo and Member of Congress. He died on the 8'h day of February, 1872.

Jeheil H. Halsey was appointed July 22, 1837 as Judge Birdsall's successor. He died December 5, 1867.

John Morgan who was appointed surrogate March 2, 1843, was the last surrogate appointed, he serving until July 1st 1847, at which time the offices of the county judge and surrogate were consolidated and the duties of each performed by the county judge.

This concludes the Judiciary of the County of Seneca from the foundation of the county to the present but it does not seem right that I should conclude this paper without referring to the Hon. John Maynard and Addison T. Knox who were long residents of this county and held the position of Judge of the Supreme Court which was not part of the Judiciary of Seneca County any more than of other counties comprising the Supreme Court District in which they presided.

Judge Addison T. Knox was the son of John Knox and the third in birth of seven children; he was born in a house near the "Kingdom". He was a cripple from birth and as his mother often remarked "Being a cripple Addison always had his own way and that is the reason he has such an overbearing disposition." Judge Add Knox as he was familiarly called was elected in November 1859; he was an excellent lawyer and proved himself an honorable and competent judicial officer. He died May 11, 1862 and Hon. James C. Smith of Canandaigua was appointed his successor.

Judge Maynard was elected June 1847 and served until March 24, 1850 being the date of his death. And Judge Henry W. Taylor was appointed as his successor, March 27, 1850.

Prior to May 23, 1884, moneys belonging to infants and others were left with the Surrogate of the county for investment and the surprising part is that they were never required to render an account for those moneys only to infants who might attain the age of twenty-one years. Simply turning over to their successors in office the money in securities which they had on hand In May 1884 an act was passed by our Legislature directing the General Term of the Supreme Court to appoint some suitable person to examine the books and accounts and vouchers of the Surrogate's Court relating to these trust funds and directing that the surrogate turn the amount so found in his hands over to the county treasurer and from that time the county treasurer and not the surrogate has been the depositary of these funds and although the surrogates were not required to render an account of these funds, yet when the accountant appointed by the Supreme Court examined the account of the surrogates, he reported all moneys were accounted for and that there never had been one cent lost in the acts of said surrogates of our county.

For many of the biographical facts contained in this paper I am indebted to Hon. Didrich Willers, ex-Secretary of State and in closing I wish to express my thanks for the help he has given me.

To the officers of this association who have honored me as their choice to prepare this paper I can only in this feeble way express my appreciation and wish that health and strength had been spared me that I might have presented to them a more acceptable paper, but I assure them that situated as I have been since I was notified of their desire I have done the best I could and hope that its contents will be of benefit to them in the further progress of their historical work.

Our Predecessors in Seneca County

The Sachem-O-ja-geght and the Cayuga Indians.

By Fred Teller.

It was an early hour of the afternoon of the 21st of October 1794 when an aged chief or Indian sachem of the Cayuga Nation arose. Before him burned the council fire of the six nations. From his place at the head of the inner circle of the council, he gazed around upon a vast gathering that encircled him as it stretched away in ever widening circles. This council was the last general one ever held by the United States with the Six Nations as a whole and it was the largest concourse of the different tribes comprising its different nations, except the Mohawks, that has ever since been gathered together. Besedes the Cayugas and the other allied nations of the Iroquis Confederacy were a number of the conquered and dependent tribe. The Senecas, however were by far the most numerous. The number in attandence amounted to very nearly two thousand red men. The treaty was held a few miles to the west of us at Canandaigua, from where the council was convened could be seen the waters of that beautiful lake sparkling in the sun surrounded by the barbaric colorings of the wild forests in their Indian summer frost tints.

The aged chief who had arisen to his feet to answer on behalf of the Six Nations the congratulatory and introductory address made by the Indian Commissioner Col. Pickering, on the day previous at the opening of the grand council was O ja-geght. He was commonly called by the whites "The Fish Carrier" and sometimes "Old Fish Carrier." He was the headsman, or chief sachem of the ten civil magistrates of the Cayuga Indians and the senior at the time of the fifty sachems who governed the civic affairs of the Six Nations. The ancient scrolls of parchment with the wampum attached that are now in the custody of the Regents of the University of the State of New York are the original state treaties that released to the State of New York the lands that compose the present county of Seneca. These are the title deeds to the lands that are our birthright and upon which have been built the homes of ourselves and people for one hundred years. If you will examine the signatures with the totums and sign mannels attached thereto you will find on the part of the red man that the first name in all cases by reason of his rank, his standing, and his seniority signed to them to be O ja-geght.

Of the means used by the Commissioners of the State of New York to persuade, cajole, circumvent and to almost forcibly wring from the Cayuga Nation and from this unlettered man O-ja-geght their lands it is the purpose of this article to treat. To this savage barbarian who stood out alone against our sovereign state and whose one voice making conformation impossible almost blocked the treaty that completes our chain of title to the beautiful rivers and vales, glades and lakes, on which are built up the communities that we here to-night call home, your attention is asked.

Before listening to the remarks of this Cayuga chief or sachem we will better understand them if we go back to February of this same year 1794 to a council that was a preliminary of this the larger one. It was called at the instance of the Federal Government at Buffalo Creek for the purpose of conciliating the feelings of the Cayuga and Seneca Indians One of the serious questions that confronted the young "Republic of the Thirteen Fires" as they were called by the Six Nations was the Indian problem. The vexed question of boundary lines had settled down into a stern determination on the part of the allied Indian tribes of the west, that the Ohio river should mark the utmost white frontier settlements. In this they were openly abetted by Thay-en-da-naga (Joseph Brant) the fighting chieftain of the Mohawks and his entire Mohawk following. This powerful nation who had esponsed the cause of the British in the Revolutionary war had retired to Canada on lands assigned to them by the crown after the Revolutionary war on the Peninsular northwest of the Niagara river. Many of the young men and warriors of the Cayugas and Senecas were also upon the warpath in the west. Gen. St. Clair had been defeated in a pitched battle on the Miamis and it was desirable to prevent the Cayugas and Seneca Indians from joining the belligerents en masse. These efforts however were crowned with but partial success.

The government distributed on this occasion a liberal quantity of presents including clothing. The place of meeting so near the frontier of Canada was such however that it was largely under the control of British officers. Col. John Butler of Wyoming memory was conspicuous in his endeavors to thwart the designs of the United States commissioners. Joseph Brant and Red Jacket were the principal speakers. After much discussion of numerous propositions it was adjourned with the idea of calling a general council to be held later in the year. Rumors were accordingly sent out summoning the entire Six Nations to a council to be held at Canandaigua in the following autumn. This great and memorable council which convened was the result.

In the meantime the State of Pennsylvania prepared to extend her settlements to Presque Island on the shore of Lake Erie. This greatly exasperated the Six Nations who claimed this territory as exclusively their own. The Six Nations were about to take the

field under the leadership of Joseph Brant when President Washington in terferred and prevented Pennsylvania from any further prosecution of her designs at that time.

The Indians commissioners appointed to represent the United States at Canandaigua were Col. Pickering called Con net sauty by the Indians and General Israel Chapin. The last named was a great friend to the Indians and upon his death the following spring a council was held in honor of his memory April 28, 1795 at which a request was made that his son Captain Israel Chapin might be appointed in his place. There were also in attendence at this council by special invitation of the Indians, six quaker friends, three from each Pennsylvania and New Jersey. The Onidas who were the first to arrive on the 11th of October went into council upon matters pretaining exclusively to their own nation. On the fourteenth the Onondagas and Cayugas arrived and on the same day Ho na ye-wus or Farmer Brother arrived at the head of a large delegation of Senecas.

They were received by the Indians dressed and painted with all the brilliancy and beauty of their wild fantastic tastes. On the 18th Sa-go ye-wat-ha or Red Jacket and Ga hio-di-euh or Cornplanter and several other Seneca chiefs arrived each with large delegations.

On the afternoon of the 18th the commissioners and friends were summoned by a son of Cornplanter to attend the formal opening of the council. The officers and their interpreters were surrounded by a dark assemblage as the council fire was kindled and the pipe of peace went around. The Indians are very deliberate in council and it was not until the 20th the business of the council really began.

Upon that occasion Col. Pickering performed the ceremony of condolment with the Delewares for the loss of one of their braves. He, in words, took the tomahawk from the head of the victim who had been murdered by a white man and covered the grave with leaves so that no one could see it in passing. The hatchet which he had taken from the head of the victim was buried beneath a pine tree which *in words* was torn up for that purpose. Having placed the hatchet in a deep hole and covered it over with stones, the tree was replanted on top so that the instrument of death could never be discovered. The colonel then wiped the blood from their heads and the tears from their eyes and opened the path of peace which the Indians were invited to keep clear at one end and the United States at the other as long as the sun shone.

It was for the purpose of answering this address of Col. Pickering of which the above was the preliminary that on behalf of the Six Nations, O ja geght had arisen in the council. Drawing the blanket around his tall and erect though aged form with all the natural grace of a native Indian he addressed himself to the commission on behalf of his countrymen. The national government has preserved nothing in its archives in regard to this council except the bare treaty itself. But from other sources, a portion of the outline of the interpreter's remarks have been saved. After delivering the belt of wampum by which he had been summoned to the council.

He gazed retrospectively at the relations that had existed between the intruding white man and the Six Nations "When the white man first came and landed on our shores the Indians saw that they were men and must have something to subsist upon. They therefore pitied them and gave them some land and when they complained that the land had become too small for them the Indians still pitied them and from time to time gave them more. Tidings were carried back and still more came among us, yet we did not fear them. We took them to be friends for they called us brothers. At length a great council fire was kindled at Albany where a silver chain was made which was kept bright for many years until the United States and the Great King over the waters differed. Then their brothers in Canada talked to the Indians and they let the chain fall out of their hands, yet it was not

their fault but the white people for this land over which our white brothers quarrelled was created by the Great Spirit for the use of his red children.

In the war that ensued the minds of our people were very uneasy. We were unable to agree and our council was divided. A part of our people stood by the council of the thirteen fires while the greater portion held fast by the treaty belts which were held by the King across the great waters. He referred bitterly to the abandonment of her Indian allies by the British at the close of the war and that in the treaty of peace no provision of any kind had been made for them. He recapitulated the history of the negotiations with the whitepeople afterwards and referring to the treaties of Fort Stanwix complained of the many grievances they had suffered particularly in the curtailment of their territory. The Indians felt that at the first treaty at Fort Stanwix in 1784 the commissioners had been too grasping. In the subsequent treaties every effort had been made to fleece them of their lands until now "we have hardly a place left on which to spread our blankets but still you are not satisfied." In concluding O ja geght stated that notwithstanding their many causes of complaint now, that they had taken hold of the chain with the fifteen fires he pledged the Six Nations to hold on.

In the above speech O-ja-geght complains of the curtailment of the lands of the red man by the various treaties. Let us take up the treaty of 1789 by which most of the lands composing the present county of Seneca were released to the state. The exception being the lands of the west Cayuga reservation bounded on the east by Cayuga Lake, north by the Seneca river, west by the reservation road and south by the town of Romulus.

It was determined by the State of New York to hold a council with the Indians in September 1788 at Fort Schuyler and agents and runners were sent out by the New York Indian commissioners to induce the Indians to attend. It was intended to make this as imposing as possible and great preparations were made for this embassy to the Indian country. I shall quote almost liberally from an article of the late Geo. Conover. The board of commissioners and their retinue started from Albany on the 23rd and did not arrive at Fort Schuyler until the 28th of August. A wild romantic scene was soon presented Governor Geroge Clinton pitched his marquee and was surrounded by man y who had been conspicuous in the Revolution and were then leading men in the new state. They were surrounded by the camp-fires of the numerous representatives of the Six Nations amounting to thousands. Indian traders were there from New York and Canada in large numbers with their showy goods and trinkets and fire water, ready for the sale of goods on the espousal of either the interest of the s'ate or the lessees. Prominent lessees from Albany, Hudson and Canada were in the crowd secretly and insidiously endeavoring to thwart the object of the council, hearing that one of their principals John Livingston was present. Governor Clinton ordered him to leave in three hours and retire to a distance of forty miles.

The lessees were a company who had leased from the Indians a considerable portion of their lands for a term of 999 years. The laws of the United States and the State of New York prohibited the sale of their lands by the Indians without the approval of the government and the state. To evade this the lesses had leased nearly the whole of western New York for the above term which practically amounted to a sale. The prominent lessees were John Livingston and Dr Benton. Their object was the creation of a new state west of the reservation line similar to Vermont which had recently been split off from the eastern part of New York and been admitted to state hood.

"Governor Clinton finding that the Cayugas and Senecas had held back sent messages to Kan a de saga now Geneva, to hurry them forward. They found Dr. Benton a prominent lessee and his agents surrounded by Indians

dealing out liquor and goods persuading them that either New York would cheat them out of their lands or else put them to death. Many of them were undeceived and started on the journey but so great had been the beastly intoxication, that but few went further than Scaw yace (South Waterloo) being to unable proceed and but few reached the council, one Cayuga dying on the road."

On the 9th of September the council was opened by a speech by Govenor Clinton and after a few days negotiation, a treaty was concluded with the Onondagas whereby all their lands were secured except certain reservations. Negotiations with the Oneidas followed and after some days a like treaty was procured from them. The council had now continued for twenty five days It became now important in order to secure the balance of the Indian lands to procure a treaty with the Cayugas and Senecas. Rev. Samuel Kirkwood was despatched to these tribes to inform them what had been done and to prepare the way for a council.

Seth Reed and Peter Ryckerman who were both noted Indian traders located at the Indian village of Kanadessga were engaged to aid in getting the attendance of the Indians at Albany. Both of these traders were committed to the interests of the lessees, the lands and set off to them by the state commissioners in this treaty which aided n securing will show how they came to change their minds. Reed and Ryckerman responded as soon after these arrangements had been completed as possible. First sending James Manning Reed to Albany with a letter saying that they would be in Albany the latter part of January with the Indians and adding that the lessees kept the Indians so continually intoxicated with liquor that it is impossible to do anything with them. It was not until February 1889 that Ryckerman was able to collect a sufficient number of Indians and reach Albany.

The council was accordingly opened on the 19th with the Cayugas and some Onondagas and Oneidas being also present. None of the prominent Cayugas either sachems or warriors were present. A converted Cayuga Indian known as Good Peter or Dominic Peter was the principal speaker for the Cayugas. Present at the council was a considerable number of their women whom Good Peter called governesses and of whom he said, "Our ancestors consider it a great transgression to neglect the council of the women, particularly the governesses whom they consider the mistresses of the soil. They said, who brought us forth? Who cultivate our lands? Who kindle our fires and boil our pots but the women?

On the 25th of February, 1789, the treaty of Albany was concluded. In the first two clauses of this treaty they ceded and granted to the State of New York forever all their lands except the east and west Cayuga Reservations containing one hundred square miles, exclusive of the waters of Cayuga lake and the place called Skayes on the Seneca River and a competant piece of land on the south side of said river at the said place sufficient for the said Cayugas to land and encamp on and cure their eels.

The third clause gives the Cayugas and their posterity forever the right of hunting in every part of said ceded land and of fishing in all the waters within the same.

The fourth clause names the consideration on the part of the state which was $5,000 in silver (the receipt whereof the Cayugas do hereby acknowledge) and a further payment the following June 1st at Fort Schuyler of $1625 00 and an annuity of $500 per year. The state settles with Peter Ryckerman in the same clause for his share in procuring the treaty by paying him out of lands set aside for the Cayugas as per the following clause— and as a further consideration to the Cayugas the people of the State of New York shall grant to their adopted child, Peter Ryckerman whom they have expressed a desire shall reside near them, to assist them and as a benevolence from them the Cayugas to him and in return for services rendered by him to their nation, the said tract of one mile square at the Cayuga Ferry, excepted out of said lands reserved to the Cayugas for their own use and cultivation. Ryckerman was also granted in the fourth clause of the treaty 16,000 acres of land adjoining and on the west side of Seneca Lake, surrounding a house lately erected and now in occupation by the said Peter Ryckerman. There is excepted out of this 370 acres which were granted to a white man who married a daughter of a Cayuga named Thynowas. It was Ryckerman's endeavor to beat his partner out of any participation in this land that has placed so many documents on file at Albany and given so much light on this treaty.

The closing four lines of this treaty were evidently added to mollify if possible somewhat the known hostility of O ja-geght to releasing any of the lands of the Cayugas to the state. They read as follows. Notwithstanding the said reservation herein above specified, to the Cayugas, it is declared to be the intent of the parties that the Cayuga called the Fish Carrier shall have a mile square of the said reserved lands for the separate use of himself and his family forever.

The signatures to the treaty are remarkable on the part of the red man from the fact that it is signed by but fourteen Indians and twelve governesses. Nine of these signatures were signed by but one Indian Kun is tagia whose mark is a steel trap. The peculiar marks and totems are interesting. Besides Governor Clinton and Lieutenant Governor Van Cortland on the part of the state are Ezra L. Hommedieu, Abram Ten Brock, John Hathorn, Samuel Jones, Peter Gansvoort and Egbert Benson.

There was great indignation on the part of the rest of the Cayugas as soon as it was known that a treaty had been entered into and negotiated by so small and uninfluential a part of their nation. As soon as the runner with the tidings of this treaty arrived at Tey o heyhoco ls (Buffalo Creed) where quite a number of the Cayuga warriors and chiefs with their followers were in camp for the winter immediate preparations were made to return to this neighborhood. The feeling was very bitter and ranked very strong in their minds that the Cayugas had not been treated fair in the matter of this treaty. O-ja-geght at the head of his people drove the surveyors from their lands, destroyed the stakes and refused to be oppressed. Every means to pacify him was without avail. When the first day of June came it was felt to be a vital necessity that the signatures of some of the more prominent warriors, chiefs and sachems of the nation should be secured to an article ratifying the treaty of the previous year. It seems that on the 22nd of June this fact was accomplished for we find on that date the Cayugas had come forward to Fort Stanwix and received their annuity and also the further sum of *one thousand dollars as a benevolence* and we the said Cayugas in consideration thereof do by these presents fully freely and absolutely ratify and confirm the said agreement and cession. This was signed by twenty-four Sachems, chiefs and warriors of the Cayuga Nation of Indians. The first signature being O-ja-geght alias Fish comer, the next Shogovegh watha or Red Jacket, and the names of the leading men of the Cayuga Nation follow, omong the leading witnesses was Joseph Brant. W. L. Stone in his life of Brant speaks of him as having been a great and life long friend of Ald chief of the Cayugas. New York refers to the 1789 treaty as having been made at Albany on that date and confirmed by subsequent articles made at Fort Stanwix, June 22, 1790.

Their reservation on the east and west shores of Cayuga Lake were soon surrounded by settlers. Leases were made to the whites in some instances and in others squatters swarmed in and took possession. By reason of their lease of ferry privileges to John Harris and James Bennett, a highway was opened which was travelled by all who made use of the ferry. There was another class, the felons and outlaws who sought refuge there. There was

a provision in the treaty by which the state bound itself to clear the reservation from intruders on said reservation without the consent of the said Cayugas and the Cayugas on their part to the State in the apprehending of intruders, felons and offenders to the end that they may be brought to justice. It was necessary on a number of occasions for the state to summon a sheriff's posse to clear and drive out by main force the intruders, so that the Cayugas could retain and enjoy the residue of the lands that remained to them.

The treaty of 1789 was no sooner ratified in the following year than longing eyes were turned to the fair lands that yet remained to the Cayugas. It was not long before interested parties who afterwards obtained a share in its distribution began to talk of—as the treaty afterwards negotiated states—"make the lands of the said reservation more productive of annual income to the Cayugas." It was not until July 27, 1795 that commissioners on the part of the state concluded a treaty at the Cayuga Ferry whereby the Cayuga Nation released to the state all their lands except two small reservations on the east side of the lake.

It is not the purpose of this article to go into the details of this treaty as it was touched on in the article on the Early Ferries and the Genesee Highway, the Samuel and John Harris and two additional articles entitled the Cayuga Treaties soon to appear in the Grips History. The negotiating and concluding of the treaty met the determined opposition of O-ja-geght and it was not until a1 of his followers had been won over and he had stood out alone for many days that it was consumated. The mile square reserved to O-ja-geght in the 1789 treaty he evidently refused to release as per this clause in the treaty "one other piece of land one mile square at 'Canoga' for the use of an Indian sachem of the said nation called Fish Carrier and for the use of his posterity forever."

The two small reservations of two miles and one mile square on the east side of Cayuga Lake were by treaty purchased by the state on May 30, 1807. The reservation containing the Indian spring and village at Canoga secured to O-ja gegh was exchanged for an annuity of $50 per year. This was paid to his heirs up to August 2, 1841 when by Chapter 234 of the laws of that year it was extinguished. O ja-geght was an old man at the date of the 1789 treaties and after the loss of so much of their lands he lived most of his time with the Mohawks in Canada. He however afterwards visited a number of times the territories that for three centuries had been the homes of his people. He was present and signed the treaty of 1807. There is a tradition that during a subsequent pilgrimage to the graves of his people at Canoga he died. The name and sachemship is still kept up among the remnants of the Cayuga Nation.

The Cayuga Nation of Indians were one of those composing the Five Nations After the adoption of the Tuscaroras who were a conquered tribe speaking a similar dialect whom these nations found in North Carolina into their confederacy it became more widely known as the Six Nations. This league was called by the French the Iroquois and was the most powerful and widely known of any of the Indian tribes on the continent. In the fanciful and figurative language which they made use of they termed their formation ('Io-di-no-sau-nee, the long house) which signifies a long house having partitions and separate fires. This was the ancient way these people had of building their bark houses large enough to accommodate a number of families.

The home domains of the Six Nations stretched the entire length of the Empire state. The first fire the extreme western one was the Senecas. They were known as the hill people and were the fiercest, the most populous and furnished the most warriors and warchiefs. They were designated as the keepers of the western gate. The fifth fire at the east end was the Mohawks and they were the guardians of the eastern door. On this tribe devolved the naming of a warchief and the collection of tribute was one of their

duties. The third fire was the great council fire of the Six Nations and was in charge of the Onondagas. The council fire was put out when the Onondaga council house was destroyed by Count Frontenac in 1696. It was again put out in the spring of 1777 and again for the last time in 1779. It was never afterwares relighted in the old place in the council town. Of the fifty sachems who governed the civic affairs of the Six Nations, fourteen belonged to the Onondagas. The head or chief sachem was with them the name To do-do-ho and the title going with the office, also the Ho-no-we-na-to or national wampum keeper was an hereditary office that was confined to the Onondagas. The wampum represented the history of the nations which was talked into it.

One of the interesting features at the unveiling of the Red Jacket Monument at Canoga on October 14, 1891, was the presence of Chief Sachem Skanawati the official keeper of the wampum belts or records. He exhibited a large wampum belt and explained its use and the manner of keeping the records of the Confederacy.

The second fire was that of the Cayugas. They were the custodians of the Ah-so qua-ta, the peace pipe. The Cayugas were designed at the council fires as the So-mus-ho-gwa-to-war which signifies the great pipe. In addition to the apple and peach orchards and clearings of corn were large fields of cultivated tobacco surrounding the Cayuga castles or settlements. It was their right to apply the lighted brand from the council fire to the calumet at the national council. The smoking of the peace pipe and the passing of it around the circle from hand to hand was the preliminary or formal method of opening all councils. In the general council it went first to the Onondagas and came around to the Cayugas last in whose keeping it remained until the next council. The rudely drawn figure of a calumet placed opposite the names of their chiefs was their official signature and it was their totam and their insignia as a nation.

Upon one side of the council fire

were hung the Onondagas, Seneca and Mohawks for they were the fathers of the league, on the other side were the Cayugas, Oneidas and Tuscaroras for they were brothers but children of the first three. The Cayugas were formerly a part of the Seneca nation at some remote time in the dim recesses of tradition in which the early trail of the Cayugas are lost. When the Seneca hunting grounds around the Genesee became too thickly settled for easy subsistance a band under the leadership of some favorite chief migrated to the outlet of Cayuga lake. In time they grew in numbers and became distinct. They were formerly known under the title of the Gwe-u-gwek-o-no which means the people of the mucky land. This referred to the Montezuma marshes where their first settlements were made. The Oneidas in a like manner were originally a part of the Mohawks and became a distinct nation in a similar manner.

Few who to-day occupy the lands that formerly belonged to the Six Nations realize the extent to which they carried their conquests outside of their home territories. The limits of this paper will admit of but one extract or two from well known writers.

Morgan in his league of the Iroquois says, "No frightful solitude in the wilderness, no impregnable recess in the frozen north was proof against their courage and daring. By the year 1700 they had subdued and held in subjection all the principal nations which occupied the States of New York, Delaware, Maryland, New Jersey, Pennsylvania, Virginia, Ohio, Kentucky, Northern Tennessee, Illinois, Indiana, Michigan, a portion of the New England states and a principal part of Canada. Over these nations the haughty and imperious Iroquois exercised a constant supervision.

Chauncey M. Depew in his centennial address at the hundredth anniversary of the State of New York referred to this incident. A tribe of Manhattans had sold some of their lands to the white settlers without the consent of the Iroquois, this was contrary to their agreement. A single Mohawk

warrior was sent as an envoy to attend to it. Summoning the offending tribe to a council he asked to have the Chief that was responsible for the transaction pointed out to him. He thereupon buried his tomahawk in his brain scalped him and hanging his still bleeding scalp to his girdle strode out from the terrified and submissive assembly."

DeWitt Clinton says of them, "They were the Romans of the west. Their conquests if we consider their numbers and circumstances were not inferior to that of Rome itself. They ran in conquest further than the Greek arms ever carried and to distances which Rome surpassed only in the days of its culminating glory.

On November 6. 1768 the boundary line between the Six Nations and the State of New York, New Jersey, Pennsylvania, and Virginia was fixed by a treaty at Fort Stanwix between the officials of these states and the Six Nations, on behalf of ourselves and of our several dependent nations. The Cayugas signed by their seal or totum the crude drawing or picture of a calumet.

The Cayugas though situated far inland were so favored by nature that they could by several water routes that centered in their territories quickly assemble and go forward on the warpath in any direction. Their remote, secluded territories on the other hand in the midst of a stupendous forest scenery would seem to be the original abode of sylvan happiness. Their principal villages, settlements and encampments were on both sides of Cayuga lake. At the Canoga Springs was their village of the name Ca-no geh signifing, oil on the waters. The Spring was considered by the Indians to be possessed of medicine properties and capable of driving away certain evil spirits that brought disease. Red Jacket was born near this spring somewhere about the year 1750. His mother was a Cayuga. The order of descent in Indian lineage was through the female line and although the father was a Seneca the son of the mother was a Cayuga. You will find his name signed to most of the Cayuga treaties. His title to the wolf clan was from his mother and though called by some writers a prince of the turtle clan because his father was of that clan, an Indian would never call him so. In the mile square reserved to O-ja geght were a number of their burial places. The Indian has always had a great veneration for the graves of his fathers and it was a reproach to the Cayugas that they did not retain even a place to bury their dead.

Another village of the Cayugas was Ge wa-ga means a promintory running out. It was on the other side of the lake near Union Springs A little further south was their principal village where the council house of the Cayuga Nation was situated, Ga-ya-ga an'-ha which means inclining downward. It is said it refers to the reflection of heaven's dome in the waters, another Indian word more fully expressing it being Ga o ya-di-o, where the heavens rest upon the earth. On the site of Ithaca was Ne-o dak he-at meaning at the end of the lake. Where Aurora is situated was De a-wen dote, constant dawn. The Cayugas were the keepers of the southern gate of the Confederacy, a place where all the rivers and trails came together Ta- yo ga, at the forks. These names show that the Cayugas were not insensible to their beautiful surroundings.

Their name for the Seneca River was Swa-geh, flowing away. This was the name of the river from Seneca lake until it empied into Lake Ontario. Coming up the river however it was the Onondaga until Onondaga lake was passed Cayuga river until Cayuga lake was passed and then Seneca River This point on the Seneca river where we are gathered tonight was the carrying place or portage. It marked the somewhat elastic boundaries between the Cayugas and Senecas. The site of Seneca Falls was called Sha-se-once which means swift flowing or tumbling waters. As the principal trail of the Six Nations also ran east and west through our village it is probable that there has never been a time since the Indians inhabited this country that there has not been a collection of bark cabins, tepees or wigwams of this migratory race scattered through the forests on either side of the river at this point. Numerous evidences were found here of former Indian occupation.

Scoy yase west of us seems to have been a cosmopolitan settlement composed of migratory bands contributed from all of the Six Nations. These as they journeyed east or west on the trail or carried around the rapids pitched their habitation, tarried for the fishing or social interchange. There was always as a consequence encampments all along the river.

Here in this very heart of nature along these beautiful streams and around this land locked expanse of mirrored waters dwelt our predecessors the Cayugas happy under the smile of the Great Spirit. The waters were teeming with fish and the forests with game. They chase alternated with the council. Ho-di os seh they called them which signifies advising together. There was their local festivals and observances as well as their general gatherings at the Onondaga council house. "If for instance the Cayugas lost a sachem or chief, a runner was sent out with belts of invitation to the sachems of the league and the peoples at large to assemble around their council fire. As soon as the runner had reached the trails of the Onondagas it was taken up by them and circulated through their nation and one of the Onondagas fastest runner took up the message and passed it on to the Oneidas and they in a like manner to the nations at the east. In the meantime another Cayuga runner had reached Can a di sa-ga the chief Seneca's village and was it being circulated through the Seneca's villages by their runners. The belts and strings of wampum sent out conveyed a message. The name of the deceased calls for a council.

The name and appeal fell not in vain upon the ears of the Iroquois. There was a potency in the name itself which none could resist. It penetrated every seclusion of the forest, and reached every Ga-no-soh hunter upon the hillside, on the margin of the lake, or in the deep solitudes of the woods. No warrior, wise man or chief failed to hear or withstand the call. A principle within was addressed which ever responded, respect and veneration for the sachems of the league."

For these councils, and the festivities with which they were concluded the Ho de-no-san-nee ever retained a passionate fondness. No inclemency of season, nor remoteness of residence, no frailty of age or age of sex offered impossible obstruction. To that hardy spirit which induced the Iroquois to traversethe warpaths of the distant south and west and to leave their hunting trailsupon the Potomac and the Ohio, the distance to the council within their immediate territories would present no considerable hinderances. From the Mohawk to the Genesee they forsook their hunting grounds and their encampments and put themselves uponthe trail for the council fire. Old men with gray hair and tottering steps, young men in the vigor of youth, warriors inured to the hardships of incessant strife, children looking out upon life for the first time and women with their infants enclosed in the ga-oo-ha, baby'frame, all performed the journey with singular rapidity and endurance. From every side they bent their footsteps toward the council, and when the day arrived, a large concourse of warriors, chiefs, wise men and sachems, from the most remote as well as the subjacent parts of their territory, greeted each other beside the council fire of the Cayugas.

There was one peculiarity of the council only that the limits of this article will permit calling attention to and that is the ruling of the majority over the minority. No majority could force the minority, that would be the curtailing of their liberties. They must all be, as they expressed it, of one mind, otherwise everything fell to the ground. When the Six Nations went into council in regard to supporting the British in the Revolution the Oneidas could not be brought to agree with the majority. Hence all were at liberty to do as they pleased. This was true in the treaty of 1795 ceding to the state the Cayuga Reservation. Had O ja-geght refused to go with the majority the treaty could never have been ratified.

People or classes of people seem to leave their footprints upon the country they inhabit. East of us the Puritans left theirs, "upon the stream and rock bound coast" where first they landed. Nearer the Dutch left theirs about the Hudson, a lordly yet a sleepy going region. About and around Cayuga Lake has always rested a benign, pastoral, restful presence. It breathes of hospitality and the open door of welcome. The summer clouds that curl like a halo above it ever seem like the vaporings that had just left the bowl of the As-o-qua-ta, the calumet, the peace pipe of the Cayugas. Peace and sweet content have ever hemmed it in.

Thy surface wide, a glass,—transparent bright
The farther shore like rainbow tips fades blue
In tender tints of a celestial hue
You bark like cockle shell so frail and slight
Suspended floats; blank space and bright
The rich toned shadows fashion it again
Reversed beneath thy burnished plain,
Submerged wide heavens down so snowy,white
Draws magnet like each shade of natives soul,
Fields square of meadow, hills of mossy turf
The woodland mass, the tree trunks gnarled girth
The worlds sharp struggle to some selfish goal
Floats off beyond horizons utmost knowl
Becalmed lies every joy that is of heaven or earth.

When the hazes of Indian summer mantles our lovely lake, the fair Cayuga wraps her robe of royal tyrian purple about her. Its shades and tones are such as the most lordly potentate of the east might envy.

Their insignia that the Cayugas ever kept suspended from the ridge pole of their bark cabins or hung ever at hand in the folds of the wigwam still casts its spell. Like a white winged benediction the calumet curls its incense above us. Ga-o-ya-de o, the heavens rest very near the earth. Almost all we can hope for when we reach that golden shore that lies beyond earth's troubles lies spread before us here. Peace quiet rest.

NOTE—The limits of this article will not permit of the inserting of a quantity of material relating to O-ja-geght There are a number of extracts from the diary of Thomas Morris (son of Robert Morris) giving a minute description of some interesting ceremonies at Tioga Point, over which O ja geght presided, and his (Thomas Morris') adoption into the Six Nations, also to the delegates of the fifty chiefs of the Iroquois to Philadelphia at the instance of George Washington and their subsequent conference with O-ja-geght at Buffalo Creek; all pointing to the great influence exercised by him over the councils of the Six Nations, neither can any reference be made to Logan and other influential chiefs of the Cayugas without making the article too voluminous.

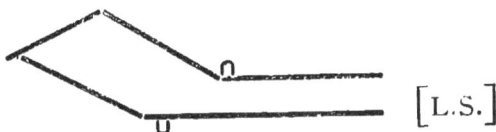

$$[\text{L.S.}]$$

The Seneca Falls Fire Department

BY MAJ. PRYCE W. BAILEY.

Although the village of Seneca Falls was incorporated April 22, 1831, there are no records obtainable of the transaction of any business under that act until the year 1837.

Previous to 1832 it is presumable that the fire protection of the village consisted wholly of the bucket brigade. Sometime in that year, according to the memory of our oldest fireman, Mr. James Sanderson, the reliance on the bucket only was, as decided by a few of the energetic citizens of that day, an ineffective fire department for such a thriving community as Seneca Falls. So a few of these up-to-date young men managed to procure from somewhere an engine of a very primitive sort, as measured by the seeming perfect engines of this day, no more so, perhaps, than ours will appear to our successors seventy years hence.

This engine was a square box with, what appears to have been from the description, a rotary action pump set inside it, and from which a shaft extended outward to each side of the box; windlass cranks were attached which were operated by the firemen. The rising main of the pump was a flexible leather tube with a nuzzle on the top end. The captain stood on the box and directed the stream toward the fire. The water was carried to the machine by the bucket men, or women; the box being filled, the crank men would pump until it was emptied, and rest while it was again being filled. This operation was repeated until the emergency was passed by the complete consumption of the structure.

The officers of this fire company were Captain, Henry Wolsey; Lieut. Charles L Hoskins, brother-in-law to the Captain and father of Mr. L. S. Hoskins; Dr. Thomas Swaby, a brother of the late Dr. W. A. Swaby, was a member, A. N. Beardsley was also a member. As a matter of note there were no "city fathers" to provide a home for, this powerful engine, so it was, that, after the fire had consumed all property within reach and the firemen had patted each other on the back in congratulation over the excellent service each had done and the bucket brigade weary with their exertions, all repaired to their homes leaving the engine where it was last used. Perhaps on the following day a fireman more interested in the machine than were his fellows, and possibly, with more time than they, would drag it into some backyard, there to remain until again wanted to frighten a fire and kindle enthusiasm.

All freeholders were, by law, required to keep on hand, for fire uses, a number of leather or wooden buckets, proportionate to their assessment on the tax roll, and on an alarm being rung were to report at the fire with them whether in day or night. At the fire two lines were formed, one, the males, to pass up the buckets, the other, the females to pass back the empty ones to be again filled from the river, wells or cisterns as the case required.

On the south side of Fall street there were a number of residences, where now is the block of stores; these were lower down than the present sidewalk line, and their sole water supply for all uses was the river; the water was drawn up by rope, bucket and windlass For the north side of the river, both business and residential part, this was the source from which water for fire protection was obtained. The engine, after a fire on the north side of Fall street, had been put, by the aforesaid interested one, in one of the backyards in the rear of a cow stable and, in the course of time and the usual process of cleaning, the inside of the stable, the engine became completely buried under a warm coat of manure. About this time, one boisterous windy evening the firemen were congregated in one of the few village grocery stores, when one observed that this would be, or was a bad night for a fire, and suggested that it would be well to lo k for the engine; when Dr. Tom Swaby spoke up saying, "Give yourselves no uneasiness on that account gentlemen, for I already have two men with dung forks hired to go, in case of fire, and dig out the engine as soon as the alarm is given." With this assurance, the party gave no further thought to the tempestuous night nor to the possibility of danger arising therefrom. This state of fire department affairs presumably continued for the following four years.

The charter adopted by the Board of Trustees in January of the year 1837, provides for the organization of a fire department. Article 53 of that instrument authorizes the Board of Trustees to require the inhabitants of the village to provide and keep ready for instant use a specified number of fire buckets.

Art. 54 says that the board shall procure fire engines and other apparatus for the extinguishment of fires and provide fit and secure houses and other places for keeping and preserving the same; and they shall have power to organize fire, hook. hose, ladder and axe companies; to appoint during their pleasure, a chief engineer, and two assistant engineers of se department, and a competent number of able and reputable inhabitants of said village firemen to take the care and management of the engines and other apparatus and implements used or provided for the extinguishment of fires; also to make rules and regulations for their government; and to impose such reasonable fines and forfeitures upon said firemen for a violation of the same as they may deem proper; and, for incapacity, neglect of duty or mi-conduct to remove them and appoint others in their place.

Art. 56, Every fireman who shall have faithfully served as such, in said village including as well as any period before, as after the passage of this

act. ten consecutive years, shall be hereafter exempt from serving in the militia, except in case of war, invasion or insurrection; and the evidence to entitle such person to the exemption, as provided in this section, shall be a certificate under the corporate seal signed by the president and clerk.

In July 1837, the board authorized and accepted the organization of Fire Engine Co. No. 2, to consist of forty able and respectable men and by resolution appointed William H. Arnett, foreman, and Charles L. Hoskins, clerk, the following named persons were chosen firemen: James B G. Downes, John W. Dickinson, William R. Goetchins, John T. Andrews, W. A. Sacket, Henry Hayden and Edwin M. Conklin. These constituted the nucleus of a large and efficient fire company not No. 2 Engine Co. only. but also of the present splendidly equipped department of our village.

The intended organization of a large department was clearly indicated in the adopting of the articles of the charter, in the appointment of a chief engineer and assistants and defining their duties, specifying the time for the election of company officers. placing the companies under the command of foremen and providing for the suppression of insubordination by the imposition of a fine of eight shillings for each offense reported to the board by the chief.

"Sextons of churches and watchmen of shops were appointed firemen, who when a fire occurs, to repair with all haste to the churches and shops and diligently ring the bells thereof until the danger is passed." Six persons from the firemen shall be appointed Axe Men, to take charge of the axes, and, on presentation of a certificate of the foreman to the effect that they have good axes, the board shall pay each man twelve shillings They are to attend at all fires with their axes and shall, be under the direction of the trustees and fire wardens, or any three of them, They shall cut down and remove any building, erection or fence for the checking of the progress of the fire. Any axe men failing to

48

attend with his axe or refusing to
obey the orders of the officers in command shall pay a fine of $1 00. Axe
men are exempt from cleaning committee and working on engines.

A further expansion of the department, was begun by the board in 1838,
to the extent of detailing a sufficient
number of men from among the firemen to take the care and management
of the hooks, ladders and implements
for aiding in the extinguishment of
fires. They shall be exempt from
other fire duties but shall be under
the command of a foreman. The
above implements are to be kept in a
secure place designated by the president, and shall be inspected once each
month by the chief engineer

The companies as above designated
shall be known as Hook & Ladder
Co. No. 1, Axe Co. No. 1, Engine
Co. No. 2. All companies hereafter
organized shall take numbers next
above in their order.

All citizens, when a fire occurs in
the night, are ordered to place a
lighted candle at the front door or
window of their residences, where it
shall remain until the fire is extinguished and the firemen return.

Any person who may repair to a
fire, shall be obedient to the orders of
the chief engineer in the extinguishment of fires and removal of goods.
A refusal to obey will be punished by
the imposition of a fine of five dollars
($5.00).

At fires a trustee shall wear a white
band on his hat. The chief engineer
shall wear a leather cap painted white,
with a gilded front and the word
'Chief' painted thereon. He shall
also carry a speaking trumpet painted
black, with "Chief" painted in white
thereon.

A foreman of an Engine Co. when
on duty shall wear a black leather cap
with white front piece with the word
"Foreman" and number of engine
painted in black thereon.

A foreman of the H. and L Co. shall
wear a cap like that prescribed for
engine foreman, with number of company and his initials on front piece.

A foreman of a hose company shall

wear a cap like that prescribed for H.
& L. foreman.

A foreman of the axe company shall
wear a cap like that prescribed for H.
& L. foreman except that an axe shall
be painted in black on the front piece.
It is made a duty of the chief to report
all violations of these ordinances to the
Board of Trustees.

Constables are required to watch
out for fires and to give alarms,
keep the street numbers of the chiefs
and their assistants conspicuously posted
in the watch house; and when an alarm
is sounded notify these persons at once;
also to watch the premises after the
engines have returned to their houses
after the fire is distinguished.

By resolution of the board, George
H. McClary was appointed chief engineer in the year 1837. Mr McClary
who had the honor of the first appointment as chief was a noted manufacturer
of that day and owned and conducted a
foundry and machine shop on the property now occupied by the Ingersoll
paper mill.

The No. 2 engine was purchased
from Lewis Seelye, a builder of these
goods at Rochester, N. Y. The engine,
Hook & Ladder, Axe and Hose companies were housed on a lot owned by
Ansel Bascom, situated between the
Seneca House and the ravine on Bayard
street (opposite the present house of
No. 3 steamer.) Mr. Bascom stipu-
lated that the house was to be moved
off if the lot should be sold.

Ansel N. Beardsley was appointed
foreman of the combined H. & L and
Axe companies in August, 1837. One
month later Silas Hewitt was made a
fireman and appointed foreman of the
above combination, vice Beardsley, declined. During the year 1837, the following named were appointed firemen
and attached to No. 2 Engine company.
James A Adair, Joshua Martin, Geo.
Edson, John Knerr, William P Pollard,
Charles Lowry, Frank P. Latham,
Jacob Clark, H. C. Silsby, Stephen
Bishop, William L McKee, John H.
Wheeler, O. A. Campbell, C. S. Hoskins, O. C. Watson, H O Clark,
George Hocknell, Ira A. McBain, Alfred S Miller, J. B Johnson, George

Stecher, Jacob H. Corl, George Hall, John Crosset, W. S. Finley, P. Van Ness, Ira Stockman, Seth A. Thomas, Richard Stradder, E. J. Thomas, S. B. Westcott.

In June 1838, the Captain of No. 2 was authorized to procure a hose cart for his company; this is the first mention of a vehicle for this purpose. The small quantity of hose that had been in use was carried on the engine; but when Captain Arnett was ordered to purchase 150 feet of new hose at a price not to exceed $180, it became necessary to have a more convenient place than the deck of the engine to carry it.

In order to meet the expense of this unusual increase of the department the following gentlemen advanced $10.50 each: Ebenezer Ingalls, William H. King, Silas Keeler, Henry Wolsey, C. L. Hoskins, William L. Gaylord, J. Bennett & Co., Edward S. Latham, Shelton Wood, Mathias B. Bellows, John S. Gay, Garrett V. Sacket. They were reimbursed with interest.

The hose cart was made by Van Ness & Willet at a cost of $34.00. The tax budget for this year has an item of $100.00 to be raised for the improvement of the fire department.

In March of this year George H. McClary was removed from the position of chief engineer and Edward S. Latham was appointed to the vacancy. In July, 1839, Samuel Reeve, W. B. Lathrop, William Cain, Henry Seymour, Obadiah Latham, W. P. Gaylord, D. Sacket, were appointed firemen of No. 2 Engine Co.

In September a motion prevailed in the board of trustees to disband the H. & L. Co. until suitable and proper apparatus is obtained, and George Hocknell was appointed and authorized to procure proper implements for the company. They seem to have been procured by Henry Hocknell at a billed cost of $23.69.

Ira Stowell was appointed to the H. & L. Co. and Wm. E. Williams to the Engine Co.

The H. & L. Co. seems to have been a troublesome member of the department from the day of its organization.

In February of the year 1840, J. S. Bristol was appointed to make a thorough investigation of the H. & L. and report. His report was probably an oral one, for in this same month there were additional bills to the amount of $102.65 presented and paid for, on account of H. & L. wagon. Captain Hewitt was directed to find a place to store the present unfinished and imperfect wagon and implements.

In November of this year Edward S. Latham and George H. McClary were appointed as a committee to have the H. & L. wagon completed and procure a house for it. The committee did its work and the wagon was housed near the Franklin House.

In February of this year, 1841, the following bills were audited and paid: Edward S. Latham to material and labor, H. & L. house, $44.46; Silas Hewitt to ladder, $3 00; C. D. Mynderse, to ropes, etc., $16.88.

In January, 1842, the H & L. Co. is ordered to parade with its apparatus on the first Thursday of each month, and is required to put its apparatus in good serviceable order under pain of disbandment. The result of these orders we find a resolution passed by the board in July, disbanding the H. & L. Co. and its members be given certificates for the time served.

This year marks the extinction of one company and the birth of another. On the 25th of July, 1842, Rescue Engine Co. No. 3 was organized for the purpose as given in the application of its officers to the board of trustees for acceptance, "to aid more effectually in carrying into operation an act establishing a fire department in the village of Seneca Falls."

The names presented to the board were R. G. Noyes, Arza L. Burrit, Jas. Sanderson, Jr., Wm. H. Arnett, C. Kenyon, George R. Chase, W. B. Maynard, Charles Platten, John W. Conklin, David R. Gould, Chas B. Keeler, Isaac VanTassell, Thomas Carr, John Leach, John C. Lace, Geo. A. VanCleef, Wm. Keith, James Dennison, Bayard Miller, Wm. Clark, F. J. Mills, Stephen Baker, Alfred Wood, H. J. Elliot, Wm. Langworthy,

50

Washburn Race, D. C. Bloomer. J. V. Chamberlain, A. E. Chamberlain, I. H. Arnett, John H. Davis, O. S Latham, James N. Underhill, H. Quackenbush, M. H. Chrysler, James Bellows, D. V. Sacket, John Miller. Clarence Twist, A. K. Townsend, F. F. Carr, Edward Mynderse, David Cole, E. J. Tyler. Walstein Failing, M. J. Smith, Isaac Pitcher, W. Magary, C. E. Wheeler, Peter A. Dey, Eugene Herndon, Barney Travis, J. H. Cool, Joseph Osborn, Henry Carpenter, S. D. Woodhull, Smith Briggs, C. C. Coleman, Gabriel Scott.

This company was accepted by the board of trustees and an engine house was established on Canal street in the rear of the Baptist church. A little later the company was reorganized and strengthened, and, by resolution of the board an offer of $435 was made for the engine house. The next move toward properly housing the company which was made was the appointment of a committee consisting of Silas Hewitt, O. S Latham and J. P. Fairchild to select a proper site for a house in the 2nd ward (at this time the village was divided into two wards, the north side of the river being the 1st). A site was selected by this committee near the southeast corner of Bridge and Bayard streets. A house was built thereon, costing $288. Mr. O. B. Latham was the builder.

As before stated, the engine No. 2 was built by Lewis Seelye of Rochester ;so No.2 wanted a machine equally as good and, if possible, a little better. So in May 1844 the board asked for an appropriation of $500.00 to pay for a machine. William H. King was appointed, a committee to inquire into the merits of engines now made; after receiving Mr. King's report, the president was authorized to contract with Mr. Seelye for an engine like that he had built for No. 2, at a price of $860. The chief engineer is again ordered to inspect the H. & L outfit and report its condition. In April, 1845 is made the first mention of a reservoir, this is in a resolution of the board appointing a committee to notify Mr. Asa Fuller of the faulty condition of

the one built by him in the first ward. Reference is also made to a hydrant at the Stone Mill through the payment of the bill of William Burtless for repairing it.

Again in June, 1845, George Hocknell and J. W. Dickinson are appointed to examine the condition of the hooks, poles and ladders of the H. & L. outfit. Birdsall Holly, the inventor of the eliptical rotary pump and engine which contributed more largely to making Seneca Falls a world wide celebrated fire apparatus building village, than any other event, was appointed a fireman in September 1846.

In October 1847, President J. K. Brown and Jr P. Fairchild were authorized by the board to purchase a lot for No. 3 engine house and to contract for the moving of the house.

At the annual meeting of the department, William H. Arnett was designated chief and was instructed to use his influence with the board to induce it to accept the H. & L. Co as a member of the department.

In May, 1848, $40.00 was appropriated for the two engine companies, to be paid in quarterly installments of $5 00 to each company. It is to be justly presumed that this pittance was to cover the cost of the supplies only.

During this year, No. 3 went through the process of reorganization for the purpose of weeding out the worthless members. The records show that, during the six years of its existence, it had performed a deal of arduous duty under many discouraging conditions, such as non-attendance at the regular meetings, the impossibility to collect fines and dues from the negligent and insubordinate members. So it was resolved to disband and reorganize under the following pledge, to wit. "We the undersigned do hereby agree to live up to our code of by-laws made for our internal government; and we do further pledge ourselves to be guided by them in all cases, initiation, fines, etc. etc, Thomas Carr, E. Norcott, Byron Beebe, D C. Bloomer, E. J. Tyler, George Hall, C. C. Brown, James Bellows, William Wilbur, C. C. Coleman, W. H. Foster, Walton Jones,

51

Charles J. McKee, James II. Underhill, George Stevenson, John F. Wheeler, C. B. Keeler, Jr., II. Hadley, R. Aspell, Thomas Lusk, T. J. Crosby, William Crawford, Robert R. Perry, E. Crawford, Charles Twist, Samuel A. Stevenson, II. W. Seymour, Henry Bellows, John Leach, William Gunn, Bradley Miller, Leonard Egleston, William Arnett, Walstein Failing, G. R. Chace, A E. Chamberlain.

A new uniform was adopted as follows: Hat of glazed oil silk, red flannel shirt, dark trousers with India rubber buttons.

No. 3's records. "We were challenged by No. 2 and we beat them to death." Thus giving evidence of the effect of the recent re-organization and the weeding out of the company all of the unserviceable material.

In April the taxpayers meeting voted $100 for contingent fund, and $150 for new hose, and directed Chief Arnett to sell all old hose and apply the proceeds to the purchase of additional new hose. In July the No. 3 engine was moved to a lot on Cayuga street, a part of the Daniels property, and adjoining what is now Story's storehouse.

Again in April of this year, 1850, an appropriation of $200 is asked for, to be applied to the purchase of a new H. & L. wagon.

The recently adopted new charter makes it obligatory for the chief and his assistants to see that H. & L. apparatus is always in order for instant use; also to command at all fires until the flames are extinguished; and they are empowered to compel obedience on the part of all subordinate officers on pain of suspension of the offender and to appoint one to supersede the suspended one and report his action to the board at its next meeting.

In June of this year the chief was ordered to report the condition of No. 3 engine, state its requirements for putting it in good serviceable order; this report was evidently made at once because at the next meeting of the board he was directed to send the suction hose of this engine to New York to be repaired. In August the suction hose

was received repaired at a cost of $59 75. So we are left with the impression that the engine was deprived of its suction hose for at least one month.

In March 1851, Carlton W. Seeley was paid $12.50 for barn storage of the H. & L. outfit. A committee consisting of Messrs. Thomas Carr and James Bellows made an oral report of the present condition of that apparatus that was continuously rising to trouble the board.

The brothers, Henry and Perry Stowell were appointed firemen in April 1851.

In June, 11. W. Seymour and Bellows were appointed to inquire into the condition of the fire department fund in order to ascertain whether it would warrant the purchase of new hose for the engines.

In September Thomas Carr superceded W. 11. Arnett as chief of the fire department.

On October 12, 1852, the whole fire department turned out to attend the funeral of Stilman Brim, a brother of A. W. Brim.

In February, 1852, the H. & L. company, or rather, the outfit, comes up again in the appointment of a committee to ascertain the approximate cost of putting the implements in order for use; in response to the report, the committee is empowered to procure ropes, etc, and provide a building to keep them in.

In June, 1854 the Board of Trustees relaxed its tight grip on the money bags and voted the magnificent sum of $50 for the proper celebration of Independence day by the fire department.

A special tax meeting was called in this month, in response to the prayers of a largely signed petition, for the purpose of voting the sum of $2,800 to be applied to the purchase of two first-class, 12 inch cylinder, engines with all modern improvements, and 1,000 feet of best quality hose. As a matter of course the appropriation carried with a rush, because, at about this time, the active rivalry of competing builders of fire engines, had given a sudden impetus to a spirit of strife for excellence on the part of the fire companies throughout the country, by the presenting of cheap prizes to be competed for, with their engines. So, the firemen of Seneca Falls desired to be put in possession of nothing short of the best, and, as the spirit of strife was rampant, the companies increased their membership until they embraced the adult male population of the village.

The necessity for properly organized and drilled hose men became more apparent, and action was taken by the board ordering that twenty men be detached from each engine company and drilled as hose men by a competent officer. This action of the authorities led to the forming of a hose company in April, 1854, which was named Yankee Hose Co. Its first foreman was Charles J. Martin, who held the position a short time and was succeeded by William H. Pollard.

In August, 1850, the Continental Engine Company was accepted by the village and was designated "Continental No. 1." This company took the better of the two old engines.

The two new engines made by Button & Co. of Waterford, N. Y., were delivered in August and were accepted provided certain necessary alterations were made in them. The president was then authorized to order from Button & Co. two hose carts at a price of $298 for the two, if three trumpets for the chief and his assistants could be gotten in the transaction. We got the carts.

For the following two years the trustees were seemingly kept busy auditing bills for alterations and repairs to the engines and hose carts, but all such bills were charged to the account of Button & Co. and were presumably allowed by them in the final settlement.

In February, 1856, $100 was voted for a reservoir fund. The chief was directed to ascertain if the old red storehouse could be rented for Continental Engine Co. This company had taken the old engine of No. 2, and the president was requested to advertise the No. 3 engine as for sale. In May of this year E. J. Tyler was ordered to

purchase 200 feet of good hose for No. 1 from Button & Co.

In October Chief Lucius C. Gibbs, father of the late ex-senator Gibbs, ordered out the three engine companies to play for prizes. At this home tournament No. 1 captured the first prize by running with their engine twenty rods, attaching the suction hose and throwing water through fifty feet of hose in 1 minute, 25 seconds. This was considered an excellent exhibition of the celerity of action and perfect drill of the company.

H. W. Seymour was appointed chief vice Gibbs who had left town in November. On December 28, 1855, the whole department turned out to attend the funeral of ex-chief Gibbs, who had been accidentally killed at Whitehall, N. Y.

On February 12, 1856, in tax meeting the citizens voted an appropriation of $200 for reservoirs and ordered that two be built during the year.

In May of this year the old No. 3 engine and the village hearse were put up at auction sale. J. H. Cool bought the engine at $100. There being no one present who thought he needed a hearse it was not sold.

In August, 1856, E. Edson was awarded a contract to build two reservoirs at $70 each.

Continental Engine Co. was authorized to have such alterations made in their engine as will permit the water to be taken in at the front part of the machine.

In September, in preparation for a great water throwing tournament, so called, the three engines were put in the best possible condition at Cowing & Co.'s works, which had Mr. H. W. Seymour, a thorough fireman, as superintendent.

Following the improvement of No. 1 engine it became necessary to increase its membership for although the engine was classed as No. 2, its cylinders had been enlarged to such an extent as to be but 1 8 inch less in diameter than the first class engines, so the company presented to the trustees for acceptance the following list of names: George Stevenson, Wm. W. Norton, C. B.

Randolph, Charles Parker, J. M. Gifford, T. J. Robinson, R. Ridley, B. F. Peck, A. S. Auld, Thomas Bartuett, C. B. Brusie, Hiram Almy, George Niles, John Youngs, Randolph Hewitt, John McArthur, Charles Davis, L. W. Fisher, Wm. VanKirk, Charles Rinker, Peter Feeck, jr., Maynard Stout, Oscar Moore, George Cowing, J. Y. Churchill, C. W. Coleman, G. A. Schyler, William Wilson, Garrett Bogart, J. S. Moore, Lewis Tripp, R. Miller, Henry Manwarring, Richard Curran.

On August 22, 1857, it is recorded that, the annual meeting of the fire department was held in Good Templars hall of the Woodworth block, northeast corner of Ovid and Bayard streets.

In April 1858, the No. 3 engine house was rented to a Miss Sanborn, to use as a school house, for six shillings per week.

An annual department meeting was held in Concert Hall, now Ryan's furniture repository, on August 22, 1858, for the purpose of selecting a chief; because of some disagreement, Captain W. R. Goetchius of No. 2 marched his men out of the hall. Those remaining elected Jacob II. Corl to the position. Corl declined to accept. The situation regarding the matter was reported to the president who then appointed Edwin J. Tyler to the place. Tyler filled the position for two months only when Simon W. Arnett was appointed to fill out the remainder of the year but who filled the place acceptably until 1867.

On October 6, 1859, the department consisting of "Continental" No. 1, "Seneca Chief" No. 2, "Rescue" No. 3 and Yankee Hose No. 1 passed in review before the president and chief, and afterwards gave exhibitions in water throwing, and returned to their quarters; in the evening had a grand torch light parade.

A report of a committee made to the Board of Trustees relative to the purchase of the "Livery Stable" premises, which had been made by the board of the preceeding year, showed that a lot could be purchased and a brick engine house built thereon for $800 less than

the livery stable purchase could be fitted up for. The committee recommended the repudiation of the purchase and that the amount now paid be charged off to profit and loss. The matter was referred back to the committee with instructions to make the best terms possible. The affair was amicably settled after a time. The livery stable referred to, is the old building on the east side of Bridge street opposite the Franklin House barn.

Soon afterwards a lot was bought for $175 by the committee, and the foundation for the future building, and the reservoir 25x18x5 1-2 deep was contracted for $169 and the work advanced with rapidity. On February 5, 1860, Silsby, Mynderse & Co., submitted to the trustees a proposal to furnish the village a small steam fire engine, to be drawn by men for the sum of $2,500 and also proposed to furnish an engineer to run it at fires, and keep the engine in repair for one year for an additional sum of $150. Both propositions were submitted to the annual tax meeting which was held in March, and both the bids were accepted; and a further appropriation of $885 for "department maintainance was voted. In May, the steamer was delivered. The trustees ordered that it be kept in the house of No. 1, and that engine companies Nos. 1 and 3 be consolidated into one company of sixty-seven men; and the No. 2 engine offered for sale.

In November 1860, No. 2 engine company disbanded and gave up their engine to the village after an eventful existence of twenty three years.

On the morning of January 21, 1861 Captain W. R. Goetchius was found drowned in the Dey race near the present location of the Climax Specialty Co's Works. He had been the foreman of the No. 2 engine company for eighteen years. He was a model fireman of those early days, faithful to every trust, loyal to his comrades and a vigilant, indefatigable foreman who preferred the captaincy of his company to promotion to a higher grade to which he had many times been urged.

In March of this year, the trustees recommended the appropriation of $3,100 for the purpose of building two engine houses, one on each side of the river; but the recommendation was not favored by the taxpayers and it was voted down.

In May 1861 the Board of Trustees resolved to issue exemption certificates to all firemen who volunteer for the war; this was the practice for the succeeding four years.

In August 1861, a company was organized and accepted under the name of Excelsior Hose, No, 3. The following named persons composed the company: John Arnett, Theodore Pelham, Patrick Burns, Owen Burns, M. McCabe, M. L. Waldo. William Burns, Michael Knight, D. T. Kneath, Thomas Mackin, Edward Riley, Patrick Sullivan, R. Sawyer, Thomas Markey, Thomas Yoe, Thomas Mc Grain, Joseph Adams, Charles Marshall. The life of this company was a short one. A majority of the members were in the army or navy inside of six months after the company was organized.

In October the department turned out to attend the funeral of Corporal McClure, a member of a recruiting squad for the regular army, who had been murdered in the village.

In February, 1862, the board formed a plan to raise $2,000 from taxes and add to it $1,500 from the general fund for the purpose of building a brick engine house on the north side of the river; four months thereafter a contract was let to Edward S. Latham to build a house in accordance with plans submitted by him for the sum of $1,691.

In April, 1863, a contract was let to Kirby & Van Gorder to build a brick engine house on the south side of the river for the sum of $1,289; as a reservoir and foundation for this building was already made. The No. 3 engine company, Henry Churchill, foreman, took formal possession of this house in August, 1863.

In November, 1864, Chief Thomas Carr reported to the trustees that he had sold the No. 2 engine to the village of Groton, N. Y., for the sum of $500.

A third attempt to maintain an H. & L company was made in January 1866, by appointing twenty men for this purpose to serve under the command of the foreman of Yankee Hose, No. 1. From this time to 1868 there was no extraordinary activity, nor many changes in the department.

The year 1868, was a busy year caused largely by a series of supposed incendiary fires. In February of that year the authorities voted to purchase a second steamer which in July was delivered to the No 3 company. It was christened "Phoenix." James Desmond was appointed engineer. In order to be up to-date and in readiness, a bed was ordered for the No. 3 engine house and the engineer was supposed to occupy it. All of this preparation and precaution was followed up by the offering of a reward of $500 for the arrest and conviction of the person or persons who had burned so many buildings. One person was caught in the act of setting fire to the building across the canal from the Phoenix Mills, but the meshes of the law were too large to hold him for conviction. But the incendiarism was checked.

In January 1869, a movement was made to consolidate the engine and hose companies to forty members, in order to increase the efficiency of the department, and, at the same time reduce the expense of maintainance. This movement seems to have awakened some insubordination in the department which, in April brought out a report, from a special committee of trustees on fire department affairs, which concluded with a recommendation that the volunteer organizations, in so far as the steamer companies were concerned be abolished, and a paid fire department of two companies be established and maintained. The committees report was accepted and its recommendations were adopted by the trustees.

By authority of the board, President H. C. Burt bought the house and land adjoining the No. 3 house for the sum of $546, and ordered a barn and stable for the horses which Messrs. Hoag and

Jewett had bought for the department, built thereon.

In 1871 Moses Rumsey bought the old No 3 engine for the sum of $450. On October 1, 1874, the "Red Rover" Engine Co. was organized as a part of the village fire department to operate in the part of the village called "Rumseyville" only, except in emergencies, provided that the authorities turned over to the company the old engine, hose cart and hose. John McBride was chosen president, William Walker secretary ahd O. F. Cole foreman. Forty-seven men joined the company. From this time the company grew until it embraced a large portion of the male adults of the village who had not previously earned exemption through service. In 1884 it changed its name from "Red Rover" to "Gleason Fire Patrol." In 1886 the authorities of the village ordered the members who resided east of Walnut street, to. in case of fire, report for service on No. 1 Steamer.

On February 25, 1890, the Gleason Fire Patrol disbanded.

About 1880 the Rumseyville Hose Co. was organized with Henry Frutig as foreman and the following membership: Wm. Lallon, B. Woolidge, John Merriman, Wm Bradley, Wm. Cook, Geo. Feeek, B. F. McBride, Wm. Binney, F. Holmes, Charles Walbers. Alfred King, C. Wamby, Wm. Rupert, George Miner and Jeff. Merrigan. The death of this company is not recorded. It is probable, however, that it expired at the time of the disbandment of the Gleason Fire Patrol.

In October, of 1880, the Telephone Co. put alarm boxes in each fireman's house of the paid department. Of course as a bed was provided in the engine house of the "Phoenix," no alarm box was put in the engineers' residence. One night in November the engineer concluded to spend a night at home which proved a costly conclusion to himself and the village, for during his absence the engine house caught fire, and when the firemen arrived there the engine was cold, the house all on fire and no engineer at hand, so the house burned and the engineer was relieved. In December the village collected $1,181 from the insurance company, and John Urqnhart, the present engineer, was appointed vice Desmond, relieved.

On January 1, 1881, the company known as the Silsby Hose No 2, was organized with the following membership: Clarence A MacDonald, C. A. Reamer, Thomas Carr, Jr., Wm. Binney, Charles S. Sanderson, J. S. Hurd, George Vosburg, Russell Carter, Wm. Desmond, T. Short, Wm. Cory, J. Powell, T. Taylor, J. T. Rourk, W. E. Rupert, W. Hinckley, S Trowbridge, B A. McBride, J. Churchill, Alexander Brown, Thomas Usher and Wm. VanHouten.

Clarence Mac Donald was chosen as foreman. It was accepted as an independent company, but while their apparades was being made by the Silsby Mfg. Co., they were ordered to take quarters with, and act under the orders of Steamer No. 1 and did so until some time in 1882. As there seemed to be a redundance of hose companies, the company decided to exchange their hose carriage for a chemical engine, so on May 21, 1883, it began its independent service as the "Silsby Chemical" company. It was quartered in the Phoenix Block about where now the Western Union Telegraph office is. In 1884 it left the Phoenix block and took temporary quarters with Rescue H. & L. in the Johnson hall block. In March 1885 it returned to its old quarters in the Phoenix block. In May 1888, the first move was made in the project for building a house for its own use. On the 18th of May, a committee was appointed to select a lot, but not until December 1888, was the committee authorized to purchase the lot on Fall street, "next east of the Gardner-house," and to prepare plans for a "chemical" house. The committee promptly bought the lot. Contract was entered into with F. E Morehouse on April 10. 1889, and on December first of that year held its first meeting in the new and well appointed house. During the year 1889 the company and the village authorities were greatly exercised over a difficulty originating in the suspension of W. M. Beers, one of the company, by the village authorities. After much ill feeling had been expressed, it was discovered that the trustees, Chief engineer and the company had exceeded their powers in this unfortunate affair, one in the issue of an offensive order, and the other in too long loyally supporting an offending member, as soon as this discovery was made a compromise resulted and an amicable settlement effected. Before dropping this part of my paper I wish to say that the records are the most orderly, the most correctly kept of any that I have examined in my research. Its business has been transacted on true business principles. Of all the fire companies that have sprung into existence in the past seventy years it is the sole souvenir. Its survival, in my opinion, is largely the result of correct and legal guidance.

On April 22, 1881, was held the first meeting of a few young men to consider the advisability of organizing an independent Hook & Ladder company. The result of their deliberations was the formation of the body known as "Rescue" H. & L. This body was made up of young men of high character and standing in the community. The charter members were Charles T. Silsby, W. B. Harper, Frank Westcott, H. W. Long, W. T. Seymour, J. G. Armstrong, Charles Beh, H. N. Rumsey, Louis Maurer, A. M Bridenbecker, George B Seely, C. Mathews. W. B. Harper was chosen its first president. The popularity of this company drew out applications for membership in great numbers but only those were admitted that could pass their censorial committee. I here record the names of a few who were accepted viz George B. Davis, Ed M. Rumsey, F. W. Owens, W. B. Murray, H. C. Knickerbocker, W. C. Mundy, J H. Breslin. J G. Menges, M. D. Bellows, F. W. Davis, R. P. Lathrop, C. S. Hood, George Norton, E. W. Addison, Charles Chamberlain," C H. Williams, A. M. Johnson, W. W. Warner, R. C. Wayne, C. H. Westcott, C. W. Riegle.

In July 1881, an order was placed with Rumsey & Co. for a truck with a complete equipement to be made in accordance with the sketch and specifications submitted by the company. As it was to be a more elaborate vehicle than had been before built, much time was taken in its makeup and finish. It was delivered to the company January 2, 1882. The company records exhibit a very deep interest, in the management of its affairs, on the part of its members, for about ten years of its existence; later the interest began to lag. In 1895 it held its most successful fair ever held in our village by such an organization. In February, 1896, the inevitable appeared in the form of a resolution to disband which was adopted; and in April. Edward M. Rumsey, its president; Fred Maier, Jr., treasurer, George Norton, H. W. Long, and W. B. Harper, trustees closed the accounts of its members and dissolved. Thus ended, after fifteen years of excellent service the only successful H. & L. company the village ever held.

In June 1882, the "Ramsey Protectives" was organized and accepted by the authorities. The duties of this company were to be the protection of the goods that should be removed from burning buildings and the extinguishment of incipient fires. To this end, the equipment consisted of ropes, stakes, sledges, buckets and portable extinguishers. I give you the names of the active members: Elgar Page, George H. Raymond, Robert Gott, Byron S. Latimer, Jas. A Hibbard, Wm Hinckley, Spencer Royston, Geo. E. Lewis, Geo. H. Amidon, A. M. Hall, Geo. H. Bicknell, Walter Lewis, John H. Bilby, F. DeReamer, Chas. O. Mosher, W. T. Smith, Fred Dunham, William Nichols, Chas. Page, John Ryan, M. E Reagan, A. C Marsh Wm Sutherland, S. Woods, Harry Snellgrove, Wm Warren, John Zimmerman, John Powell, Richard Warren, Robert Warren. It was a lively, active and useful company that was richly backed by the late E. A Rumsey, after whose changed circumstances and the altering conditions in the fire department, the interest began to lag The company on November 22, 1894, divided its property among the remaining members and disbanded.

On January 27, 1887, the Bailey Hose Company was organized for the purpose of affording an adequate fire protection for the southwestern portion of the village. The organizers were Fred W. DeMott, James Simmons, Patrick Duffy, Patrick H. White, John Maley, George Stark, Joseph Campbell, F. J. Farron, Patrick Mc Guire, William H. Durnin, Owen Colgan, Owen F. Oakes, Richard Carraber, J. C. Hughes John Lacy, Thomas Dooley, J. A. Halpin, Michael Maloney who chose as officers, president, F. W. Demott; vice president W. P. McCau ; secretary and treasurer, O. F. Oakes; foreman, James Simmons.

With the proceeds of a very successful fair the company purchased a handsome combined parade and service hose carriage. After two years service as a hose company it was thought that more efficient service could be rendered with a chemical engine, so the hose carriage was sold to the village of Morristown, N. J., and a chemical engine purchased from the Holloways of Baltimore, Md.

The wisdom of the change in apparatus was clearly demonstrated on the occasion of the great fire on July 30, 1890, when the Bailey's and Silsby's chemicals worked alternately for eight consecutive hours near the Tripp house on State street and successfully checked the progress of the fire in that direction.

The quarters of the company was the brick building at the south end of the Bridge street bridge which, on the entrance of the Lehigh Valley railroad into the village, was converted into a passenger station for that road.

During its existence the company maintained a perfectly equipped fire house, having six beds, sliding pole and traps.

The bunkers were Frank J. Durnin, Horace Safely, B. F. Eggleston, P. R. Ferguson, P. H. Hughes and W. P. McCaul.

In 1898 by reason of being deprived of a home, the railroad company re-

quiring possession of their house, it was decided to sell the property of the company and divide the proceeds. The engine was sold to Gleason & Bailey who again sold it to the village of Ovid, N Y. The officers Frank J. Durnin, president; George M Casey, vice president; T. J. Coffey, treasurer; F. J Farrell, secretary and W P. McCaul, foreman. After equitably dividing the monies among the members of the company, formally disbanded.

The general village charter law under which the village of Seneca Falls is now incorporated, delegates to boards and commissioners some of the duties devolving on the Board of Trustees under the old charter. So, now our fire department is nominally under the command of the Board of Fire Commissioners which, at present, is composed of three able, skilled and enthusiastic firemen, namely, M. E. Hanlin, John Lefler, and Everett Vosburg.

The active command, as heretofore, lies in a Chief and two assistants. The present Chief Horace N. Rumsey succeeded his father, Moses Rumsey, who had filled the office for sixteen years; and has himself filled the position for eighteen years. The first assistant, M. E. Reagan probably has not a superior as an active and vigilant fireman; the 2nd assistant. Albert Sackett is fully equal to all demands made upon him in the subordinate position he occupies, and when the time comes for him to go up higher he will prove equally efficient in the higher place.

The department apparatus and fire fighting appurtenance consist of two steam engines, one hose wagon, one hand hose cart. one service hook & ladder truck and equipment, one chemical engine with a full complement of experienced engineers and hose men; 300 feet of good hose; a fire alarm system of sixteen boxes, which was installed in 1902, a water system, whose average pressure is not above 40 lbs per square inch, with eighty-eight hydrants properly distributed through the village. Each of our large manufactories is fitted with the sprinkler system and auxiliary fire pumps and hose so complete as to feel independent of village aid, but is able to greatly assist in fighting fires along the river's course.

I am informed that our department has been supplied with attachments which makes the hose of Auburn, Seneca Falls, Waterloo and Geneva interchangeable, thus enabling the engines of the four departments to be concentrated in an emergency.

All fires in their first stages are small fires; the design and purpose of the chemical is the prompt extinguishment of incipient fires; then it follows, as day follows night, that celerity of movement on the part of this apparatus is of the greatest importance. During eight-twelfths of the year our streets are in a condition to preclude the possibility of rapid movement through them by a hand drawn vehicle which weighs about three thousand pounds. What, then, in your judgment, is the remedy for this willful abridgment of the usefulness of so excellent a piece of fire extinguishing apparatus?

I give herewith a list of the chief engineers of the local fire department.

CHIEF ENGINEERS.

NAME	APPOINTED	EXPIRATION.
Geo. W. McClary	July 1837	March 1838
Edward S Latham	Mar 1838	Oct 1847
W. H Arnett	Oct 1 47	Aug 1850
Obadiah B. Latham	Aug 1850	Aug 1852
Thomas Carr	Aug 1852	Aug 1855
H. W. Seymour	Dec 1855	Aug 18. 6
H W. Seymour	Dec 1855	Aug 1856
Lucius S Gibbs	Aug 1855	Dec 1855
Lyman T. Moore	Aug 1856	Aug 1857
Eos ph M. Babcock	Aug 1857	Aug 1858
J. J. Tyler	Sept 1858	Nov 1858
Simon W. Arnett	Nov 1858	Aug 1866
Moses Rumsey	Aug 1866	Dec 1882
Horace N. Rumsey	Dec 1882	Dec 1894
Wm. B. Harper	Dec 1894	Mar 1896
Horace N. Rumsey	Apr 1896	D. clined
J. F. Crosby, acting	Apr 1896	Feb 1898
Frank Walters	Feb 1898	Dec 1899
Horace N. Ramsey	Feb 1900	

Seneca County in the War of 1812.

By Rev. P. E. Smith.

This article is mainly compiled from writings of my father, Jason Smith, and much of it had been already published in the History of Seneca County

The militia of New York consisted of every able bodied male inhabitant between the ages of eighteen and forty-five excepting those religiously opposed to war.

The report of the Adjutant-General for 1809 gave a total enrollment of infantry, cavalry and artillery of 102,068.

In 1811, there were deposits of military stores, among other places at Onondaga, Canandaigua and Batavia. The cannon at these magazines ranged in calibre from thirty-two down to two pounders.

Heavy ordinance intended for the Niagara frontier was brought from Albany on Durham boats, by the Seneca Dock Navigation Company, and landed at West Cayuga; from there they were transported on stout heavy sleds built for that purpose.

Taught by the recent war with England, the militia system was regarded as a timely precaution to guard against Indian depredation and foreign invasion. Territory was districted according to population

Privates supplied their own arms, and officers their own uniforms and side-arms. At a later date, independent companies were equipped at their own expense

Four trainings were held during the year. Two county trainings, held respectively on the first Monday of June and September; the battalion and general, held by appointments made by the field officers. Notices of musters were given, through lack of press and mail facilities, by personal visits of non-commissioned officers to each militiaman. If absent, a notice was placed on the door of the house. A failure to attend resulted in a court-martial or a fine.

The first general training in Seneca County was held at Ovid in 1802. Soon after a regiment was organized for the north end of the county at old Seauyes and out of a compliment Wilhelmus Mynderse was chosen by the troops for colonel, and duly commissioned by the Governor. Lambert Van Alstyn was Major and Hugh W. Dobbin, adjutant. Mynderse cared little for martial exercises and left the work of drilling to Van Alstyn and Dobbin, men who had seen service and were destined to win honors in the threatened war. Colonel Van Alstyn kept a boarding house in the first tavern erected at Seneca Falls later known as the Old Market. His charges were considered excessive, being never less than twenty five cents per week, and once reaching $2.63. General Dobbin lived about four and a half miles west of Waterloo, and at home and in the field was a soldier by nature.

About 1811, an artillery company was formed with headquarters at Seneca Falls. A single gun, an iron nine-pounder was drawn from the state. Captain Jacks led his company against the British and Indians during the war. The last surviver of his company was Hiram Woodworth of Tyre. He was wounded by the premature discharge of the gun he was loading, losing one eye, having his arm injured.

Anticipating a collision of arms, the Governor early in the spring of 1812, called upon the militia regiments to furnish a company each, for service on the Niagara frontier. Promptly responding Seneca sent out a company under the command of Captain Terry of Ovid. The names of the men who went from Tyre were Benjamin Marsh, Silas Barton, James VanHorn, Richard Thomas, Halsey Whitehead.

The men were in barracks at Black Rock when news of the declaration of war by the United States arrived. Hostilities were immediately opened by an exchange of shots with the British artillerymen across the river.

The regular army was augmented by forces of militia raised by drafts. The drafts were made for a period of three months. All the militia were called out in this way, and some were called upon a second and even a third time. A few fled the draft. Substitutes were obtained at thirty dollars for the three months. A private soldier's pay was five dollars per month but was increased to eight dollars. The first engagement in which Seneca soldiers took part was the struggle at Queenstown.

The Americans were led by General Van Rensselaer of Albany, the British by General Brock. The Americans crossed the river at daybreak October 13, 1812 and were successful in the early part of the day, but the British being strongly reinforced from the garrison at Fort George and the American militia being affected by the number of wounded brought over, and averse to leaving their own territory, the comparatively small force of Americans engaged, after a gallant fight, was compelled to surrender as prisoners of war. Of men in the battle from Seneca, was a rifle company raised in Fayette, commanded by Captain Ireland and a few volunteers from the militia. All fought bravely, until the inevitable surrender took place. Fully one third of the men whom Ireland led into action, were killed or wounded.

The year 1813 closed with disaster to the United States forces on the frontier. The British assumed the offensive and waged relentless and cruel warfare.

On December 19th Colonel Murray with an armed force surprised and captured Fort Niagara commanded by Captain Leonard. Most of the garrison were bayonetted, and little quarter shown elsewhere. General McClure called on the militia of the western counties of New York, to turn out *en masse* to defend Buffalo and Black Rock. A panic spread through the country. The British were reported to be crossing the river. Thousands of militia from Seneca and neighboring counties took arms and began their march to Buffalo.

Quoting from the reminiscences of Jason Smith the following incidents of that march may be interesting. He says, every man turned out who had any patriotism, whether he was liable to do military duty or not. I was not old enough to be enrolled until a short time before the alarm but I took my shot gun with what powder I had, and moulds to cast a bullet to fit the bore, and went with the rest. We went that day as far as Geneva. The citizens had poured in from every direction, a great many from Cayuga county. Every public house was filled to overflowing. We got into a tavern at the south end of the village and occupied the bar-room. There were neither chairs nor benches in the room nor conveniences for sleeping, and if there had been, we could not have slept, as there was a set of rowdies who trained all night. Among whom were Leonard Wells, James Magee, Benjamin Sayre, James Gerald from this place and Noah Morris, Garry Arnold and a number of others whose names are not recollected from Seneca Falls. They would perform what they called a war dance. They would form a ring in the middle of the floor, take hold of hands and circle round and round. They would get an unsophisticated fellow in the ring, then away back and forth, and prostrate him on the floor, raise a war-whoop and make a horrible din. All the way he could get out was to treat liberally. There was a tall writing-desk in one corner under which I crawled to avoid being run over, and tried to get a little sleep, but they hauled me out occasionally and hustled me around the room.

The officers who slept in the room above us would come down occasionally and try to quiet them and they would promise to be very quiet, but as soon as they had fairly gotten into bed, they would begin again as bad as ever.

We reached Canandaigua the next day about 3 o'clock P M. where we were met by an express from Buffalo, who informed us that the British had gone back into Canada, and that we might return home. Meanwhile the British had plundered the garrisons, and burned Buffalo.

On June 25, 1814, a command known as Colonel Dobbin's Regiment, was organized at Batavia and proceeded to the frontier. Among the officers were Colonel Hugh W. Dobbin, Majors Lee and Madison, and Adjutant Lodowick Dobbins. Two companies went from Seneca; one from Ovid commanded by Captain Hathaway, the other from Junius, officered by Captain William Hooper and Lieutenant Thomas W. Roosevelt, the latter of whom had seen two years service. This regiment enlisted for six months, and was called the New York Volunteers. These marched from Batavia to Black Rock where they were joined by a regiment of Pennsylvania Volunteers, and a body of Seneca warriors and placed under command of General P. B. Porter.

The battle of Chippewa was fought shortly after their arrival, and, all unused to the terrors of musketry fire, they did little service.

Scott's brigade crossed Niagara river on July 3d and captured Fort Erie, they then advanced upon the British who were encamped behind the Chippewa, a deep still stream which runs at right angles to the Niagara. Ripley's brigade made the passage of the Niagara about midnight of the 4th and Porter's on the morning of the 5th. The two companies lay about three fourths of a mile apart.

At four o'clock P. M. General Porter circling to the left approached the Chippewas. Dobbin's regiment was in line on the extreme left. The enemy recognizing the force as militia, boldly left their trenches crossed the stream and expecting an easy victory, moved forward, and the lines of battle soon became warmly engaged. The clouds of dust and heavy firing indicated the state of affairs and Scott's veterans were ordered straight forward. Unused to battle Porter's command gave way, and notwithstanding strenuous efforts could not be brought forward

again during the action. The enemy elated by success received the attack by Scott with coolness and the combat became furious.

Major Jessup was sent with the twenty-fifth regulars to turn the enemy's right wing. He was pressed hard, both upon front and flank but gave the order "Support arms and advance" his men obeying in the midst of a deadly fire and gaining a secure position, opened a telling return fire and compelled the British to fall back. Towsen of the artillery silenced the enemy's most effective battery, blew up an ordinance wagon and opened with heavy discharges of canister upon the British infantry advancing to the charge. The enemy gave way and were driven over the Chippewa into their works with heavy loss The battle of Bridgewater or the Cataract soon followed.

A number of days passed, and the British falling back maneuvered their force to deceive in regard to their ultimate designs and meanwhile gathered vessels and began to land troops at Lewiston, thereby threatening the capture of the baggage and supplies of the Americans.

To prevent this, Scott with a part of the army was sent to menace the forces at Queenstown. About sun down of July 25th Scott encountered and hotly engaged the entire British army. Then was illustrated the old adage that " he who fights and runs away, may live to fight another day," for Porter's volunteers advanced to Scott's support with ardor,took ground on the extreme left and in good order and with intrepidity held their position and repelled a determined charge by the enemy. Stimulated by the voices and examples of Colonel Dobbin, Major Wood of the Pennsylvania Volunteers and other officers, these raw but courageous troops hurled themselves upon the British line, and made all the prisoners taken at this point of the action. Captain Hooker was killed during the engagement, which lasted far into the night.

Samuel Harris and his son John Harris

By Fred Teller.

Prepared by Fred Teller and read by Rev. H. Grant Person before the Seneca Falls Historical Society, December 21st, 1902.

Samuel Harris, the father of John Harris, who ran the first ferry across Cayuga lake, from 1788 until the Cayuga bridge was completed, was born at Harrisburg, Pa., May 4th, 1750. In the year 1795, which was the year in which the East and West Cayuga Reservations were released to the state by the Cayuga Tribe of Indians and surveyed into lots, he, the father, removed to the east bank of Cayuga lake and patented lot No. 56 in the East Cayuga Reservation tract. This lot contained 250 acres and was immediately north of his son John's. The son at the same time took out a patent for lot No. 57, which contained a somewhat larger number of acres. Samuel Harris was an old Revolutionary soldier. His remains lie buried at the Bridgeport cemetery. On his monument is recorded the following: "He was an active participant in the stirring scenes of the old French wars. He was present at the surprise and defeat of Braddock near Fort DuQuesne. He was the decided friend of his country and her cause in the war of the Revolution, during which he was appointed captain of cavalry."

His father, John Harris, Sr., emigrated from Lincolnshire, England, in 1733 and opened an Indian trading post at the fords on the Susquehanna river, where the city of Harrisburg now stands. The histories and directories of the present city of Harrisburg, the capitol of Pennsylvania, all start from the time that the original John Harris, 1st, the father of Samuel Harris located on the site of that city. He afterward surveyed the city into lots and the city takes its name from the Harris family.

There is an old oil painting in existence, which Mrs. Philo Cowing of this place recalls, that is in the possession of one of her friends in Cayuga county, (the MacIntosh family, who are related to the Harris family by marriage), representing this John Harris tied to a tree on the banks of the Susquehanna river with the fagots piled about him as he was about to be burned and tortured by the Indians. He was rescued by a tribe of friendly Indians and lived for many years afterward a life of adventure and usefulness.

Samuel Harris named his son after his father John and it was this John Harris who came to the east shore of Cayuga lake in 1778 and ran the ferry in partnership with James Bennett.

In the course of some correspondence between Mrs. L. G. Sanford in behalf of the Daughters of the Revolution and the secretary of the state of Pennsylvania, William H. Elge, it was discovered that this John Harris was also a Revolutionary soldier. He was commissioned captain, October 14th, 1776, of the 12th Pennsylvania regiment commanded by Colonel William Cook. That this regiment was in active service and so severe was its losses on the battlefields of New Jersey that in April 1778, it was incorporated into the third regiment of the Pennsylvania line and thereby lost its identity, while many of its officers, including Captain John Harris, became supernumerary. Seneca County should be proud that two such loyal Americans should have become her citizens.

In 1789 John Harris married Mary Richardson, who was a native of Frederick City, Md. The following year, 1790, his first son was born and he was the first white child born on either shore of Cayuga lake. He was given the family name, John.

The sixth child of Captain John Harris (the ferryman) was a daughter and was named Helen. She married Abram Failing, who kept one of the leading taverns of Bridgeport. When Seneca Falls began to forge to the head in population and importance he sold out his business at Bridgeport and removed to Seneca Falls, where he became one of the leading merchants of our village. To his daughter, Miss Ella, now Mrs. C. L. Story, I am indebted for the use of a very valuable lot of family documents, data and publications relating to this remarkable family. Among other things, she possesses an old print representing the same scene referred to by Mrs. Cowing, illustrating the torture and burning of her ancestor, the first John Harris, by the Indians.

In 1790, John Harris opened the first tavern at the Cayuga Ferry. This land at that time was still owned by the Cayuga Indians. It was leased from them by John Harris and was held on sufferance. The Indians were not allowed to sell their lands without the sanction of the general government and the state. The parties who held leases from the Indians however, were afterward, when it was acquired by the state and surveyed into lots, given the first privilege of patenting the plots on which they were located.

The John Harris tavern was a place of general rendezvous and you will notice on all the old maps of the East Cayuga Reservation that all trails from every point of the compass centered at that point. Its old tap room must have been a very attractive place to the Red man. The amount of valuable fur and beaver skins that must have been traded over its bar for supplies and ammunition, trinkets and the seductive fire water came to a tidy sum yearly. Its owner soon became a man of wealth and influence in the community.

In the year 1794 the lands comprised in the present counties of Seneca, Wayne, Cayuga and Onondaga were erected into a new county known as Onondaga county and John Harris was appointed its first sheriff. At the end of his term he was elected for a second term.

In the following year the council fire for a treaty with the Onondaga and the Cayuga Indians was lighted in front of the "John Harris tavern at the Cayuga Ferry." The commissioners on the part of the state were Philip Schuyler, John Cantine. David Brooks and John Richardson. By this treaty the state secured from the Onondaga Indians the Onondaga Salt Springs and from the Cayugas almost all of their lands. John Harris' name appears on this treaty as one of the witnesses. The treaty bears date of July 27th, 1795. In the construction and equipment of the Cayuga Bridge John Harris took a prominent part and was the second named one of its incorporators, three of the other four being representatives of large land companies.

In 1801 he was prominent in the formation of the Cayuga Land Company, which owned all the land within two miles distant from the east end of Cayuga Bridge. The Cayuga county clerk's office shows a large number of transfers of lots from Nov. 7th, 1801, by this company and for several succeeding years.

In 1801 he established at West Cayuga (Bridgeport) a general store, ashery and a distillery. In 1806 he was elected to Congress, succeeding as representative of this district Hon. Silas Halsey of this county. In 1806 he was appointed a colonel of the militia. During the war of 1812 he served with his regiment at the front and as a large share of his command waived their right not to be taken out of the state, took part in several engagements on Canadian soil.

After the war he settled at West Cayuga, having acquired on May 20th, 1814, title to thirty and one-half acres of land being a part of great lot No. 5. He died in November, 1824. After the war and previous to his death he held a muster of militia at Bridgeport for a number of years. Mrs. R. C. Wayne possesses one of the gilt metal shoulder epaulets, formerly the property of the late John H. Tooker, which he wore at the training day exercises that took place on these occasions on the village green at Bridgeport. We of the present day have no idea of the importance that our forefathers attached to one of these muster day gatherings. It was one of the gala days of the year and it requires no very great imagination to picture the large concourse of people that would congregate around the taverns and the green at Bridgeport, to watch the various squads of militia execute their manœuvres, amid the applause of the spectators and the rattle of accouterments. Old Mr. Tooker, then a foeble, white-haired man, once remarked to me that he had never eaten any thing that tasted quite as good as the old fashioned ridged, training day gingerbread that was made for those occasions.

A branch of the Harris family emigrated to the state of Texas and became prominent in its affairs. Harris county in that state takes its name from this branch of the Harris family.

The First Congregational Church.

By Edwin Medden.

A majority of this church seceded from the Wesleyan church in the year 1869. The Wesleyan church general conference inserted in their discipline, making it obligatory in this denomination that no person should be a member of this church who was in any way connected with any secret society, especially Free Masons or Odd Fellows. This brought forth a division of sentiment in the denomination, as many members took the ground that Wesleyan Methodism had fulfilled its mission in the abolition of slavery. All will acknowledge that the Wesleyan Methodist church accomplished great good in that cause and that it was entitled to great credit for its noble work. On the other hand, many claimed that the conference had overstepped its authority in dictating to the churches in regard to whom it should receive as members. They claimed that this decision should be left to the local church, hence the division of the church at Seneca Falls

The people who seceded formed what is known as the "First Congregational Society of Seneca Falls." Their first meeting was in Good Templars' hall or what is now known as Pythian hall. Their first meeting to form the church was called December 6, 1869. Steps were taken to incorporate it as a religious society, December 17, 1869.

Rev. W. W. Lyle was chosen as pastor, officers were elected and plans put in operation to form and build up a strong society in this community. A Sabbath school with full corps of teachers with average attendance of two hundred was organized. Edwin Medden was superintendent, Rev. W. W. Lyle was assistant.

In the meantime arrangements were being made to secure a house of worship. A subscription was started for that purpose. The effort was not so successful as was expected because other denominations started to do the same. This, of course, lessened all amounts. If the other churches had delayed, it would, no doubt, have been a benefit to all, especially to the Congregational church.

It was thought best to build as many of our best citizens encouraged us in our endeavor. A lot was purchased from Mr. Davis for $3,500. He donated $500, thus making the cost $3,000. A house stood upon this lot; this was sold and removed for $200. Work was begun at once upon this property. August 19, 1870, the ceremonies of laying the corner stone took place. First, a council of Congregational ministers was held at the hall where the church was recognized by the council as a Congregational church in full standing. Following this, the ceremony of laying the corner stone took place. Rev. T. K. Beecher, of Elmira, delivered the address, subject, "Why am I a Congregationalist?"

The cornerstone is in the northeast corner of the tower. The following articles were deposited in the stone: 1st. a copy of the Bible, 2nd, Manual and Historical record of the Congregational church, 3rd, Memorial Jubilee medal of the Landing of the Pilgrims 250 years previous, 4th, United States silver half-dollar, 5th, fractional currency, 6th, catalogues of village manufacturing firms, 7th, village newspapers, 8th, village charter, 9th, list of village churches and names of pastors, 10th, list of teachers in public schools, members of board of education, 11th. copies of "New York Independent," "Chicago Advance" and "Glasgow Christian News." 12th, minutes of New York State Association of Congregational churches.

The church was finished and dedicated for public worship, Thursday, Sept. 21, 1871. The sermon was preached by Rev. Edward Taylor, D. D., of Binghamton, N. Y. The contribution taken up that evening amounted to $2,228. The membership at this time was one hundred and two.

After the church was finished and dedicated it became necessary to raise loan on the bond and mortgage upon church property. This business was placed in the hands of the following committee: Rev. W. W. Lyle, Wm L. Bellows and Dr. R. Dunham. The loan of $14,000 was obtained from the Berkshire Life Insurance Company, of Mass., on condition, first, that the members of the society should secure several individual life insurance policies; second, that an endowment policy of $5,000 should be secured upon some individual for the church. This amount was to be used to help cancel the debt. The bondsmen were Charles Seekell, Horace Seekell, William Bellows, William King and Edwin Medden.

The burden was heavy, for the annual interest on policy amounted to $460; the annual interest at 7 per cent on loan was $980, making a total of $1,440, aside from running expenses of the church. Speakers were secured at different times to attempt to raise the debt by subscription. The two principal speakers were Rev. Mr. Ives of Auburn and Rev. Mr. Hopworth of New York. They succeeded in raising the amount needed, but, unfortunately, a large number neglected to pay. For three years the bondsmen paid the interest on loan $980 to relieve the society and enable them to recover and pay, if possible, the amount of the loan. It seemed as if the society was doomed, but the members were united and determined to do all that was possible to save the church.

The bondsmen, in the meantime, notified the holders of the mortgage to foreclose and make an agreement with the Berkshire Life Insurance Company, allowing the bondsmen to bid it in for the society at $10,000, taking a mortgage without bond for that amount. The bondsmen agreed to pay the balance on first mortgage of nearly $7,000.

Accordingly, the church was sold by sheriff's sale at the Hong House. It was bid in by the bondsmen for the above sum and made over to the society.

After another struggle the churches of the Congregational body of New York state and several of our most prominent citizens came to the rescue. Among these kind friends were H.C. Silsby, Albert Jewett, J. B Johnson, H. W. Knight and others. At last the society succeeded in freeing the church from debt. It is so to day. Shortly after Mr. J. B Johnson in his will donated $2,000 for the support of the church. This is now invested in a parsonage. The church was freed from indebtedness July 3, 1881. The following gentlemen served as pastors for supplies to the pulpit: Revs. W W. Lyle, Mr. Fessenden, Dr. Holbrook, Mr. Smith, Mr. Kinmouth, Mr. Bell, Dr. Bradford, Dr. Peter Lindsey, Mr. Rawson, Henry Margetts, and Rev. Dr. A. W. Taylor, present pastor, who has served us eleven years.

In all the years of our financial difficulties and trial the members of the church were as a unit, working together in all that pertained to the welfare of the church and the cause of Christ. The Congregational church of Seneca Falls has won a name for faithfulness and devotion to the cause. God had been our guide in all our troubles, has been blessed spiritually. In our darkest days many were converted and brought into the kingdom of Christ. Much good, we trust has been done in God's service through the Congregational church. Though many made sacrifice to the extent of loss of property, yet God blessed them because of their loyalty to his cause. Most of the heavy burdens bearers have passed away to their reward, but the church to-day honors their memory and devotion to the cause of Christ.

The Streets of Seneca Falls.

BY MISS JANET COWING.

This subject was orginally assigned to the late Miss Jennie Wilcoxen, and her notes have been freely used in this paper.

We first begin with the map of Wilhelmus Mynderse, dated September 15th, 1825, which was a description of the State 100 acres, situated in the south east corner of the Lot 100 in the Township of Junius, county of Seneca, set off as his share in the partition of the estate of the proprietors of Seneca. The original streets were the Seneca Turnpike road or Fall street, Cayuga street avenue and State street; Canal street was laid out but not named.

A map of the village made by John Burton, surveyor, in 1835, shows all the steets of the town at that time.

Running parallel with Seneca river and directly north of it was Fall street, so named from the fall in the river and grade of the street. Extending from Fall street north, was Cayuga street, (named from our beautiful lake). State street comes next, thence Mynderse street, named for Wilhelmus Mynderse one of the original proprietors of the town of Seneca, and which was the western boundary of his land, Clinton street named after Dewitt C. Clinton, governor of the State of New York, and next is Walnut street.

East from Cayuga street, there was Boyd, known afterwards as "Pig Lane," a short street running from Cayuga to Fall, named after James Boyd. An old deed speaks of him as a "Merchant of New York."

Dey street, the great coasting region running down hill all the way to Seneca Turnpike or Fall street and named after Charles and Anthony Dey, prominent business men of the place.

Prospect street, named after Prospect hill, now traversed by the New York Central railroad. From this point, a view of Seneca Falls was taken in 1817.

Johnston street named after John Johnston, the father-in-law of the late Mr. Frederick B. Swaby, who gave this street to the village. Maple street runs north from Johnston, through the Swaby addition.

In that portion of the village known as the "Flats," are Wall street at the foot of which lived Thomas I. Paine, who operated a chandelry, and was known for his great size.

Lawrence street was evidently named after Lawrence VanCleef.

On the map of 1825 the park, the Wilhelmus Mynderse, was laid out, but not named, so between Cayuga and State streets are North and South Park streets, west from State street is Jefferson street a short street extending only to Mynderse.

Then comes Chapel, extending to the western limits of village, and John street a short street north of Chapel.

Between State and Mynderse is Troy street.

On French's map of 1856 in the 1st ward, north of Troy street, a portion of land owned by Daniels, Mynderse and VanCleef was laid out in village lots and Daniel's street running from Troy to Clinton, and VanCleef street, also running from Troy to Clinton, were named after George B. Daniels and Alexander VanCleef.

West of Mynderse was Oak street, extending to the western limit of the village, running parallel with New York Central railroad from Mynderse. Goulds No. 2 shop faces Oak and Heath streets. West of Clinton was Miller, named after Deacon Peter Miller who kept a tavern and was a deacon in the Presbyterian church.

A map of village lots made by Gilbert Wilcoxen in 1858 shows the extention of the village north of Fall and west of Walnut north of the railroad; and west of Walnut were 40 acres of land owned by J. Thompson, extending 40 rods wide to the north. Parallel with and west of Thompson's property was Rumsey street extending north from Thompson's land and cutting Rumsey were Chestnut, Chapel, Pleasant and Ridge. These streets are 47 to 50 feet wide.

A map showing extension of these streets east through Thompson's property was made in May 1876, with addition of North street at northern end of Thompson's land. South of railroad; Miller street was extended further west.

Dr. H. H. Heath's addition, orginally punchased from Wakeman Burr, ran from the river to the northern limit of the village. Dr. Heath was our oldest homeopathic physician.

The Rumsey addition, known as Rumseyville was purchased of Dr. Heath in 1858 by John A. Rumsey and laid out in lots and ran from Oak street to near the northern limit of the village. The street which bears his name runs to Fall and is continued to the river through the Fred Maier addition.

In the Heath addition was Rumsey street 49 1 2 feet wide. Lincoln 49 1-2 feet wide, named for our martyred president. Fall street is 66 feet wide at this point. Then Heath street running from Fall to Oak and is the nearest way to Gould's No. 2 shop.

A map of lots in second ward, made for the Seneca Falls co-operative building lot association, by Gilbert Wilcoxen surveyor, gave the addition of three streets running west from State street 100 feet. Porter was named after J. Porter.

Boston avenue and Butler were named after Sol.Butler, a noted colored individual of this village, who lived there. Further north another J. A. Rumsey addition gave us Buffalo and Tyre avenues, west of State.

On the south side of the river and parallel with it were Canal street and Bayard street. The latter was named for Stephen N. Bayard, one of the original land owners. Extending south from Bayard was Ovid street so named from the village of Ovid, which is sixteen miles directly south. This street divides the Third and Fourth wards.

Senter named after Senter M. Guldigns, (and should be spelled with an S.) The street runs south and east and strikes Ovid; thence Bridge, Swaby, named after Frederick B. Swaby, the pioneer of that family. Toledo, then Sackett, named from Gary V. Sackett, these last three mentoned are short streets running through to Haigh.

Williams a short street running from Bridge to Swaby. Haigh street was named after Mr. Gary V. Sackett's wife. She was Ann Haigh, was also a relative of the Swaby's. It runs west from Bridge to western limit of village. Barker, short street running east from Bridge to Ovid.

Next the J. T. Miller addition in which they have opened Maynard and Mechanic streets, which run through to Ovid. Next the 3rd Ward building lot association No. 2 surveyed by Martin O'Neil for Thomas McGovern, Sr., in which has been opened Shamrock avenue. In front of 3rd ward school house is Seneca Lane running from Haigh to Mechanic. Returning to East Bayard street, we find Spring running south to Chapin; White running south to Garden, Goodwin a short street running south to Elm, and named after Mr. H. Goodwin, who built and lived in the house known as the Tyler homestead.

Stevenson runs south from Bayard to corporation limit, was named for John Stevenson, Sr., who lived at the junction of Garden and Stevenson. It is now traversed by the electric road.

Then Green running from Ovid east Stevenson street through Tyler addition, Garden from Ovid east to Stevenson, Montgomery, a short street (connecting Green with Garden) runs through the J. P. Cowing addition, named for Wm. Montgomery, the first resident on the street. Next East ave. Canoga, Sherman and Fayette streets laid out on the Tyler additions, but not yet opened Mumford street running north from Bayard to Latham, named after Mr. S. T. Mumford who owned and built the house now occupied by Mrs. Owen W. Smyth. Washington street (originally Mynderse street) afterwards changed to Washington in honor of the (Father of his Country); runs from Bayard to Seneca Turnpike. Jay is a short street running north from Bay' rd street to Seneca street. Latham street is a part of the La'ham addition, owned by Obadiah S. Latham, running from Washington to Mumford street. Another short street off from Washington is Troup street named from Robert Troup, District Judge of the United States for the District of New York in 1798, once owner of a fifth part of the town of Seneca. This street runs over the brow of the hill and is supposed to connect with a bridge at that point. Adams street runs east from Washington to Jay street, through the J. P. Cowing addition.

The land of the 4th ward building association, formerly the Selden Chap in farm, in the southeastern part of the town, was surveyed by G. Wilcoxen and Smith in 1872. East from Ovid and perpendicular to it, running east, are Chapin street, 49 1-2 feet wide (named for Selden Chapin) Boardman street, 66 feet wide, named for Deming Boardman, Sr., and South street, 60 feet wide.

Between Chapin and South streets, running north and south and east of Ovid street are Hoag street, 56 feet wide, named for Milton Hoag, Smith street, 60 feet wide, and Hawley street, 60 feet wide, named for Charles A. Hawley, Cuddeback street, 60 feet wide, named for John Cuddeback, Davis street, 60 feet wide, named for Adelbert S. Davis. Between Board man and South streets, running north and south, is Spring street, 60 feet wide. This makes an addition of nine streets.

On West Bayard street and west of the stone house occupied by the late Wm. Van Rensselaer, the land familiarly known as "Sackett's sixty acre lot," was laid out in village lots and streets, the names of which are as follows: Van Rensselaer, Courtland, Hoster, Providence, Chicago, Baltimore, California. These streets run south to the Driving Park.

Cayuga and State streets are the widest in town Bayard comes next.

At a sheriff's sale issued out of the Court of Common Pleas for the County of Seneca, in March, 1847, against the real estate, etc., of Anthony Dey, in a description of certain pieces and part cels of land, there was one as follows: "A vacant lot on Cayuga street, north of Bunt street," I find that Bunt street leads off from Boyd street, back of the Rumsey and Silsby dwellings to the old cemetery. The lot mentioned as being north of Bunt street is now occupied by Charles Frank Hammond.

SHERIFF'S SALE.

By virtue of an Execution issued out of the Court of Common Pleas in and for the County of Seneca, to me directed and delivered, against the goods and chattels, lands and tenements, real estate and chattels of Anthony Dey, in my Bailiwick I have seized and taken all the right, title, interest and estate which the said Anthony Dey had on the 26th day of May, A. D., 1846, or which he may have since acquired, of, in and to all the lands and premises hereinafter mentioned and described, to wit: All those certain pieces or parcels of land situate, lying and being in the village of Seneca Falls, on lot 100 of Junius, now Seneca Falls, known and distinguished as lots Nos. three, four, five, six, seven, eight, nine, ten, eleven and twelve on Fall street, also Nos. one, three, five, seven, nine, eleven and thirteen on Dey street, also Nos. twenty-seven, twenty-eight, twenty-nine, thirty-six, thirty-eight and forty on Cayuga street. also, a vacant lot on Cayuga street, north of Bunt street, also the Woolen Factory lot, having fifty feet front on Fall street with Water power equal to one and a half Runs of Stone on what is called Dey's race; also lot No. thirteen on Fall street, being one hundred feet front, containing nearly three fourth's of an acre of land, on which is situated a commodious dwelling house, as the said lots are laid down on a map of said village, made by John Burton, Esq., for V. B. Ryerson, and so described on a map thereof, now on file in the office of the Clerk of said county, all of which aforesaid property

I shall expose for sale at public auction at the Clinton House now kept by David Milk, in the village of Seneca Falls, on Friday, the thirteenth day of April next, at ten of the clock in the forenoon of that day.—Dated at Waterloo, the 23d day of March, A. D. 1847.

HUGH CHAPMAN, Sheriff.
By Joseph C. Payne, Under Sheriff.

At Restvale cemetery, "at that village white and still," are four streets, named by the late Mrs. Laura Russell, viz: Sunnyside Ave., Laurel Ave., Woodlawn Ave. and Magnolia Ave.

Maplewood addition, south side of river, west part of village, west of Catholic church, surveyed by G. Wilcoxen, 1900, and laid out in streets, running parallel north and south from Bayard to Haigh, 50 feet wide.

Most of the additions surrounding the town were surveyed and laid out at different times by G. Wilcoxen, surveyor, and all the various maps of the town are supposed to be filed at the County Clerk's office.

There are now a little over thirty-one miles of streets in Seneca Falls, and if one should traverse them in a day, they would have all the fresh air and exercise the most strenuous advocates of these helps would advise.

In naming the streets our citizens showed honor both to the great men of the nation and the enterprising citizens of the town, also large cities. I will recapitulate a few: Washington, Adams, Jefferson, Lincoln, Jay, Clinton, Mynderse, Bayard, Troup, Boyd, VanCleef, Daniels, Sackett, Swaby, Heath, Cuddeback, Hoag, Hawley, Davis, Rumsey and many others.

Only three of the men after whom these streets were named are alive to-day. It has been said that the streets of Seneca Falls were originally laid out on the Indian trails, and from their irregularity this may be readily believed. So diversified is the surface that one would think them almost patterned after Rome and laid out on seven hills. There was a hill on Cayuga street, from the corner of Boyd street, Pig Lane or Trinity Lane as it is now called, to Heskins corner, where boys and girls coasted. The hill on Cayuga street near where the railroad is now (not under the arch) was many feet steeper and afforded great fun for the school children. There was a steep hill on Fall street, near the old Beehive, corner of Walnut street. Some old houses standing there now show how it has been filled in.

The hill on Ovid street, beginning at Bayard. was very steep, indeed, and has been filled in with tons and tons of earth.

Both bridges were many feet lower and the lower story of Goulds shop, when it was Andrew P. Tillman's residence, was on a level with the bridge. All over this town streets have been filled in that way, showing enterprise on the part of the people.

Hardly any of our streets are straight, they run along for a while, then vere to the right or left, according to their own sweet will. But if our streets are a little eccentric, no one will question that our goods manufactured in our numerous factories and sent to all quarters of the globe are straight goods.

Speaking of regular and irregular streets reminds one of an anecdote. A Philadelphian stopping in Boston had a great deal to say about the queer streets of the hub of the Universe. "Your streets are so crooked," said he, "that it is hard getting about. If Boston had only been laid out like Philadelphia, it would be a much finer city." "Well," replied the Boston man, "if Boston ever gets to be as dead as Philadelphia, we will try and lay her out in the manner you suggest."

So we say to all who criticise the irregularity of our streets. Seneca Falls is a live town, streets and all.

The map shows that there were plaster mills, saw mills, stone mill, sash factory, barrell factory, clock factory, paper mill, cotton factory and bleachery, Globe mill, tannery, now part of Goulds building No. 1, Oil mills, chair factory, etc., in 1835.

The map 1825 shows saw mills, grist mill, carding and fulling mill.

The following advertisement from

an old paper is of considerable interest
in connection with this subject as
showing that what is now called Water
street was originally considered a part
of Fall street.

George Shoemaker,

Dealer in Staple and Fancy

DRY GOODS. GROCERIES, CROCK-
ERY AND HARDWARE.

At the stand of Shoemaker & Co.,
on Fall street, fronting the north end
of the new bridge in the west end of
the village, will always have on hand
every article in the Dry Goods line;
Groceries of every description; Crock-
ery, a full assortment; Shelf Hardware, Nails, Rope, Stone and Earthen
Ware, &c. &c. As I have determined
to conform the prices of Goods to the
hardness of the times, *Small Profits
for Good Pay* is the motto; and qualities considered; I am not to be under-
sold by any one. Please call and
examine. Butter. Lard, Pork, Eggs,
and all kind of produce taken in exchange for goods.

JOHN SHOEMAKER & Co , at the
white Brick Mill, nearly opposite, are
at all times paying the highest prices
in cash for Wheat. Corn. Barley, Rye,
Clover and Timothy seed, &c.

Seneca Falls, May 13. 1843.

The First Baptist Church.

BY REV. S. M. NEWLAND.

In presenting this paper I desire to make acknowledgement that I am quite largely indebted to the Rev. Wm. R. Wright, who was pastor of the Baptist church of this place a little over five years. This pastorate commenced September 1873. During his pastorate he prepared a historical sermon and delivered it on the fiftieth anniversary of the constitution of the church. A copy of this sermon was loaned me a few years since by Mrs. Phebe Dye, when I first prepared for my own people very largely what I shall say to-night, and from this sermon I gather most of the items of the first fifty years' history of the Baptist church of Seneca Falls, the old records having been mostly destroyed in the fire of 1898, while in keeping of the church clerk, Dr. Lowe. But no one acquainted with the Rev. Wm. R. Wright will doubt but that his statements are correct as far as the records gave him knowledge of the early history of the church. From this sermon and a few meager records found and remembrance among the older members of the church, we learn that while there had been occasional Baptist preaching in the village of Seneca Falls previous to the year 1828, it was not until in the early spring of that year that a Baptist church in Seneca Falls took on form and life. During the winter and early spring of 1827-28, several Baptist families moved into the village and as they became acquainted with the Baptists already here, nothing more natural than that a meeting be called to see what could be done in regard to a church organization. This meeting was called. It was held in the old school house then standing on North Park street. It was on Thursday afternoon, June 5 1828. At this meeting there were present, Abner Carry, Harris Usher, L. P. Noble Polly Wheeler, Charlotte Long, Mary Ann Cross, Phebe Cross, Elizabeth Carry, Huldah Silsbee, and Harriet

Noble, ten in all. This gathering was called to order by Abner Carry. He was chosen moderator, and L. P. Noble was chosen clerk. At this meeting it was unanimously decided that it was desirable and expedient to form a Baptist organization in the village of Seneca Falls, with the view of becoming a church and erecting a church building in the near future. Such was the nucleus, the beginning of the Baptist church of Seneca Falls. On the 23th of this same month, the month of June, one by name, Oramus Allen, came to the village, and proved himself a most worthy and valuable addition to the new organization. He was a licensed preacher. He had pursued a course of Theological studies in the Hamilton seminary. He became at once active and earnest, in pushing forward the new interest, and on the 16th of July, proper notice having been given another meeting was held in the same place, for the purpose of completing the organization as a Baptist church, or as then named, the First Baptist society in the village of Seneca Falls. It is evident from this meeting that there were a great many in the community, at least friendly and well disposed toward the movement, for we find that at this meeting they elected nine trustees. The names of these first chosen trustees of the church were Ebenezer Ingalls, Harris Usher, John W. Wheaton, Jonathan Metcalf, Nathan Farnsworth, Samuel Bradley, L. P. Noble, Abraham Payne and Thomas Royston. John Metcalf was chosen president of the board, L. P. Noble, clerk, and Harris Usher treasurer. At this meeting a committee was appointed to search out and get terms for a lot suitable for a church building. On July 26th, Fannie Spear united with the association, and August 30th Theopolis Cross and Jemima Cross, his wife cast in their lot with the infant church.

Their number had now reached fourteen. At this meeting held on the 30th of August, 1828, thirteen articles of faith, and a Church Covenant were adopted; this act to all intents and pur pos-s constituted the organization of a regular Baptist church. But in order to receive the recognition and fellowship of other Baptist churches, a council represented by several Baptist churches was called on the 15th of September, 1828. This council was for the double purpose of recognizing the church and the advisability of setting apart to the Gospel ministry, Mr. Allen. Nine churches were repre sented in this council by nineteen delegates. This meeting was held in the Presbyterian church, the church having been kindly offered for the purpose. It is recorded that both the recognition of the church, and the ordination of Mr. Allen were highly satisfactory to the council. At the next convenant meeting of the church held October 25th, Mr. Allen was formally and unanimously chosen as th first pastor, while L. P. Noble was chosen church clerk and Abner Carry, deacon At this meeting Nelson Payne was re eived as the first candidate for baptism and baptized on the following day, Sunday. The pastorate of the Rev. Mr. Allen lasted a little over three years During this pastorate forty-five were added to the church by baptism and thirty by letter, and from fourteen at the beginning as constituent members, at the close of this pastorate the church reports a membership of seventy, and during this time a house of worship had been erected. It was a frame building, 44 feet in length by 36 in width. It had galleries on both sides and in the rear end. There was a basement to this building, and also quite a com manding steeple. It had fifty pews outside of the galleries and would seat comfortably 300 people. Four large pillars supported and beautified the front, facing the eas', or Center street. There had been various lots proposed beside the one selected an l on which the Baptist church now stands One on Bridge street was first selec'ed and Mr. Payne offered to give one on the

north side of the river, but the present location was finally decided upon. The lot was bought of G. V. Sackett, the consideration was $200, but Mr. Sackett subscribed $200 on the church building, so virtually the lot was his subscription to the church. The building committee consisted of Messrs, Payne, Ingalls, and Noble. This building cost not far from $2,000. It was dedicated May 30, 1830, though services had been held sometime previous to this in the bas-ment, doubtless during the entire winter of 1829 and 1830. I was not dedicated free of debt. It was a small indebtedness, only $300, but it became a sort of trouble and anxiety in after years. The seats were rented, the rents ranging from $3 to $15. This church applied and was admitted into the Ontario Baptist association of churches in 1829. The association then being wider in territory than at present had thirty nine churches with a membership of over 2,600. The Ontario association of Baptist churches met with this church for the first time in 1831. As rear as have been able to asceraiin Mr. Allen's salary from the state con 'vention was $50, from church $200, and the se nd year one hundred from the convention, t e third year he had his fire wood in addition. There is mention of a Sunday school, but whether it was a permanent organization of the church, run the entire year is quite doubtful. We find that the church at the ontset placed itself on record as a missionary church, and through the years they have maintained in quite a marked degree this standard of a New Testament church. After the close of the pastorate of the Rev. Mr. Allen, the church seems to have been without a pastor, for several months; then the Rev. John L. Latham settled as pastor, but only remained about eight months. The next pastor was Henry C. Vogell. This pastorate began in July 1833. It was ended February, 1836, lasting about two years and eight months. During this pastorate the growth of the church was quite marked, though by letter rather than by baptism, forty-nine having united by letter and sixteen by baptism, but we find that quite a number were dismissed. During this pastorate the discipline of the church was resorted to for the first time, and several excluded, so the net gain was not large. We now for the first time find positive proof from the records that a Sunday school is sustained during the entire year, with an average attendance of 30, this year 36. The church reports over $100 as its benevolences. This same year plans were adopted and an effort made to pay off the mortgage indebtedness on the church. It was an effort however, without reaching the desired results, for the mortgage debt was not canceled. These years 1835 '36, seem to have been years of great agitation concerning the temporal interests of the church. We find that during these years the advisability of building a parsonage is agitated, and it seemed an assured thing at one time, that a parsonage would be built, under a generous offer made by Abraham Payne, who then owned the tract of land through which Clinton street now runs. An agreement had been made with the trustees of the church that he, Abraham Payne, would build a substantial frame house, costing $600, above this he would make all outside necessary improvements, properly grade the lot and then deed it to the society for $600 the actual cost of the building, but a disparaging and somewhat bitter remark made by the pastor, Mr. Vogell, broke the contract, and we repeat what the Rev. M. Wright has well said, and so by this act depriving the church of a good parsonage and possibly an advantageous location in later years for a house of worship. Says Mr. Wright I have been unable to locate definitely just where this lot was situated between Fall street and the railroad, but believe it to be the lot where the Wesleyan Methodist church now stands. The basement of the church was used for a time as a dwelling place, the tenant taking care of the church for the use of the basement. Earlier the basement had been used as a school room, used by District No. 2, as it was then called. But during Mr. Vogell's pastorate it was fitted up for its legitimate use as a prayer and conference room. Following Mr. Vogell's pastorate was that of the Rev. John Jeffrees, lasting about two years, and though there were quite a number of additions both by letter and baptisms, the church but barely held her own, so many removing to other places. The church reporting at the close of this pastorate in the fall of 1838, only 78 members. But about this time Jacob Knapp, one of the most noted evangelists of that day, came to labor with the church. He was with the church about five weeks. The entire community was stirred as it had never been stirred before upon the question of personal salvation. The congregations were so large that a scaffolding was erected along the entire length of the south side of the church, some 20 feet wide. It was built on a level with the base of the windows, the windows all taken out on that side of the church, that those on the outside might be able to hear, and so scores and hundreds night after night, listened to the great preacher, seated or standing on the outside of the building. Nearly 200 conversions were reported, 56 uniting with this church the last of September and 38 more before the close of the winter months, making 94 additions to the church by baptism. As the result of these meetings, the membership was now more than doubled and that within a period of less than six months. The Sunday school reported the year before an average of 60. It was in this winter of 1839, that Rev. Zenus Freeman becomes pastor of the church. He must have been a man possessed of great social gifts, as well as a true Christian. With some rich experiences, now in the very vigor of life, he served the church as pastor three years, coming as he did in the midst of such wonderful and blessed ingatherings. Coming to a rejoicing and united people, we are not surprised to find his pastorate a prosperous and a happy one During this pastorate 115 were added to the church by baptism and 50 united by letter, and the membership reported to the association in 1841 was 237, but the growth of the

Sunday school was more marked. In 1839 reporting an average attendance of 200, and in 1840, nearly 300, with two branch schools with an enrollment of 60 each. This indeed was the golden period of Sunday school work, at least as regards numbers, in the history thus far of this church, but sad to have to report that these halcyon days were of short duration, for in 1841, the next year, we find a marked falling off, only one school is reported now and that with an average of only 200. During 1839 and 1840 we are told in the records, of the large attendance of the Sunday afternoon convenant meetings, and that in the month of August, 1840, 120 were present, and during these years the benevolences of the church kept pace with their growth; $300 as benevolence, reported in 1839 and $418 15 in 1840, the largest amount ever given in one year for benevolence by the church. Bright record indeed. Would that we could have it without a cloud, even the bigness of a man's hand overshadowing this pastorate. But alas! alas! if we would be true to the historical setting of these three years, the records force us to believe that there was zeal at times, that was not according to knowledge. The home finarces of the church, during this, the most prosperous period of her history, were most fearfully and shamefully neglected. It ever becomes the church as well as the individual, to be just before overgenerous, that she may preserve her honor and integrity. It was during the pastorate that proceedings are commenced for the foreclosure of the $300 mortgage and unpaid interests amounting now to something over $400 against the church. We are glad to find however, that the proceedings were stopped, the debt paid, one man, Geo. H. McClary, paying $270 of this amount. During the three years of Mr. Freeman's pastorate, special services were held each day by a noted evangelist.' In 1840, evangelistic services were conducted by Elder Sherdown, lasting several weeks, when more than one hundred conversions were reported, about sixty uniting with the Baptist church; and this year V.

Sullivan, a sailor, was licensed by the church to preach the Gospel. After the pastorate of Rev. Mr. Freeman, the church seems to have been without a pastor for a few months. During this time a call was extended both to the Rev. I. S. Backus and N. Baker, but for some reason not stated in the records both declined to accept. A call is then extended to Rev. E. R. Pinney. It is accepted and he remains as pastor of the church for about two years. The records show no advancement in church life, either in its temporal or spiritual welfare the first eighteen months. The discipline of the church is resorted too and during the first eighteen months, 100 are either dismissed by letter, excluded or dropped, and less than two short years before reporting as benevolences upward of $400, now comparatively nothing. In 1842, politics, and especially the question of slavery agitated the church, and in the month of July, 1842, a resolution was passed by the church refusing to admit slave holders, or their enlightened apologists, and sympathizers to their pulpit or their communion, and a little later a resolution is passed against the use or traffic of intoxicating liquors, and that unfermented wine only be used at the Communion. Early in the year 1843, the pastor, E. R. Pinny, with quite a number of the church, joined heartily in the belief and teaching, that the second coming of our Lord would take place before the close of the year. Because of this belief and teaching, special meetings were begun early in this pear, with marked results, as far as additions are concerned equaling anything in the past, but this largely accounted for, without doubt, because every sermon was now a most earnest effort to convince the hearer that Christ's second appearing, and that for the judgment of the world, would take place before the close of the year 1843. During this year not far from 125 were baptized into the fellowship of this church, and the church now reported the greatest number that she has ever reported during her history, 242 members. At a business meeting December, 1843, the church voted to censure, and if need be, discipline any church member, who should be guilty of publishing among the ungodly and worldly the business transactions of the church meetings. Keen disappointment and the false position held by Mr. Pinney and a large number of his supporters, and which they had so persistantly advocated, when the year passed away and their teachings had been proven false by Christ not appearing, as they had so positively declared he would, Mr. Pinney did not re-canvass his ground and come back to a sound Scriptural basis, or to loyalty to Baptist principles and teachings, or if having changed his views so they no longer harmonized with those of the Baptist denomination, one of whose pulpits he occupied, he should have stepped down and out at once, but no, he remained until Sunday morning, February 24th, 1844, when culminated this erroneous teaching that had taken possession of the mind and heart of the pastor, and which the church had allowed to go on unchecked On this Sunday morning Mr. Pinney entered the Baptist pulpit for the last time, having handed in his resignation the day before to take effect on the following day, Sunday. He preached a most egotistical and scathing sermon, hurling awful charges against the church, denouncing her as Babylon, all Christian churches were placed together. His text was Rev. 18:4, "And I heard another voice from heaven saying, Come out of her my people, that ye be not partakers of her sins, and that ye receive not of her plagues," and then calling upon all who were desirous of escaping impending danger and coming plagues to follow him, he seized his hat, stepped down from the pulpit, leaving the church, for the churche's good, but not until he had done the church an irreparable damage. Fifty-three members unwisely followed his example, influenced by his rash statements and went out with him like sheep without a shepherd, not knowing whither they went, and many others through the persuasion of Mr. Pinney and friends who had already gone out, left the church, and so not far from 80

members withdrew from the church as the result of this movement on the part of Mr. Pinney, and the church was compelled to pass through the greatest trial of her history thus far, and from which she has not yet fully recovered. But few churches could have borne such a trial and survived, as Mr. Pinney remained here until his death, more than ten years after, firm and unwavering in his new faith until the end, and seeking most earnestly at all times to lead as many of his former flock to accept his views as possible. After this dark page of the church history we find quite a long period, covering more than a year, when the records are silent as regards church life, and we almost wonder that the broken threads were ever again taken up and that the pulse life of the church should begin to beat; but in the late summer of 1845 a call is extended to the Rev. N. Baker, who was the pastor of the Waterloo church, to become pastor of this church, preaching here in the afternoon. Three years before, when the church was in her glory and strength, for some reason the call then extended to him was refused; but now when in her deepest humiliation, few in numbers shorn of her strength, he accepts the call. The Waterloo church is soon given up and for nearly four years he serves this church as pastor. He had very much to contend with, not only caused by the schism that had nearly wrecked the church, but also because of the bad management of the church finances. Two of the previous pastors had only been paid in part. A most faithful pastor, but with so much to contend with, but little advancement is made in the membership of the church, though much is done in bringing about a better feeling and quickening the spiritual life of the church. The next pastorate is that of Rev. J. B. Burnett. He remained only a few months, and in May, 1849, Rev. H. H. Haft is called. He begins his pastorate in June and remains until August, 1850—his pastorate lasting about four months. Nothing of great note is recorded during this short pastorate. And during the next two years, 1851-2, the records are very meager, but enough is given to know that during this time the church had at least two settled pastors, the Rev. Wm. Frary and the Rev. Wm. Leggett. Two were baptised into the church by each of the pastors. The Rev. N. Baker then supplied the church for a time During this time the records were revised, and the membership now reported is 101. A call was now extended to M. W. Holmes to become pastor, but for some reason not stated withdrawn, and Rev. J. R. Whitman, who was living in the village and a member of the church, acted as a supply for some months. In February, 1854, Rev. J. V. Pitman became pastor of the church, continuing his pastorate a little over two years, and while the benevolences of the church were considerably increased and six baptized into the fellowship of the church, there seems to have been no net gain in the membership, but a loss during these years, as the church reports in the fall of '56, a membership of but 90. In November, 1855, Rev. Ira Smith was called to the pastorate of this chuurch. Of this pastorate, the Rev Mr. Wright says of the first four months we find no record, nothing is said. We might wish we could find nothing afterwards; but not so. Gross charges of immorality are preferred against him. He is dismissed from the church. Going forth to make trouble elsewhere—settling in Kenosha, Wis , where he was excluded from the fellowship of the church and from the pastorate. Still downward, as ever must be the course of any church with such a pastor and the church now reports only 80 members. Late in the year '57, C. C. Hart became pastor of the church, only to remain about eight monts. And in December '59 Rev William Rees accepts a call from the church to the pastorate. This pastorate lasted about 3 years and was without doubt a successful one. Harmony was established while more were added to the church than in the ten years preceding, and the church now reports a membership of 116. And the Sunday school has doubled since its last report, now reporting in 1861, an average attendance of 100. It is during this pastorate that a new church buiding is agitated, but it resulted in repairing the old building at the cost of about $500. Rev. Ferris Scott was the next pastor, nominally from April '62 until June '67, or for something over five years; but of this time he was away as chaplain in the army for better than two years, so that a little over three years of actual service was given to the church. And while thirty one were baptized and united with the church there was no gain in number, but a net loss of sixteen, for after revising the records the church, in '66 reports but one hundred members. In the year '67 a committee was appointed to try and raise $1,500 for the purpose of purchasing a parsonage, but the parsonage failed to materialize; and the same in regard to a committee appointed about the same time to see if a lot could be secured for the erection of a new church building. After Mr. Scotts resignation, in '67, a call was given to two different men, but both refused to accept, doubtless on account of salary, though for the first time in the history of the church thus far, a Mr. Crane is called at a salary of $1,000 The church building was seemingly insured for the first time in 1867. It was in the fall of '67 that Ira Bennett became pastor, his pastorate lasting about three years. It was during this pastorate that the present church building was erected This building is about 45 feet in width and 72 in length, exclusive of the tower, which adds an additional 14 feet. The corner stone was laid in the summer of 1858, and the dedication took place March 4th, 1869, W. H. Maynard preaching the dedicatory sermon. This house of worship, outside of the lot, cost about $12,000. About $9,000 was raised by subscription and $3,000 was secured by a mortgage loan. As we look back over this history and note the membership of the church, only about 100. it must have been a great undertaking, calling for faith and great sacrifice on the part of this people. We may be wrong, but we think a great mistake was made in this, that such a grand self-sacrificing effort made by this people had not been to the construction of their church building on the north side of the river. As an item of interest, and causing more or less of speculation, revealing somewhat of hu man nature on at least two sides, we find that in the win'er of 1869 the Rev. Mr. Burnham, a noted evangelist, had been holding extra meetings for three or four nights with the expectation of continuing for two or three weeks at least. The house was already crowded and considerable interest manifested. When on this evening, the third or fourth in the series of meetings, an alarm of fire was sounded and quite a large number went out, which was quite natural. Whereupon Mr. Burn ham came down from the pulpit, refused to go on with the service, and early the next morning, notwithstand ing he was urged to remain, left the village. The effect can readily be imagined. The opportunity was lost, and it was not only humiliating but quite a set-back to the church. In October, 1870, B. F. Garfield became pastor of the church. This pastorate lasted a little over two years During this pastorate the house purchased in Bayard stre't at the time of the building of the church, three years before, was repaired at an expense of about $250, and came into use as a parsonage. On October 1st, 1873, William R. Wright began his pastorate. At this time the church records were carefully revised and the church reports but sixty-nine members, while the indebtedness of the church at this time, all told, is reported as $4,675, somewhat of a dark outlook. The church is assisted two or three years by the state convention in the support of the pastor, the debt is decreased somewhat and much good and lasting work accomplished during this pastorate. It was the longest pastorate of any within the history of the church up to this time— a little over five years. There were fifty-nine additions by baptism. In 1874 the pastor was assisted in a series of meetings for several weeks by his uncle, the Rev. W. C. Wright, and as a result of these meetings thirty united with the church and in '76, twenty-seven as a result of

the E. P. Hammond meetings. The membership was doubled during this pastorate, reporting at its beginning sixty nine and at its close one hundred and thirty-nine members. During the year '76 the use of the baptistry is loaned to the Congregationalists. And this year, 1876, the church was reorganiz d under the new centennial trus tec'law. In the baptisms of the year one was baptized nearly eighty-eight years of age, without doubt the oldest person received by baptism during the entire history of the church. And this year, 1877, the church reports: Valuation of church property, $15,000 mortgage debt, $1,000; floating debt, $2,000; enrolled in the Sunday school, 168; church membership 121. In the year, 1878, the church votes to loan its baptismal robes to both the Presbyterian and Methodist societies. The mortagage debt of $1,000 now coming due at the close of '77, and the church having a floating debt of $2,000, it is voted to mortgage the church property for $2,000, $1,000 to pay off the old mortgage and $1,000 to pay on the floating debt. The choir about this time was moved from the gallery to its present position at the left of the pulpit. There seems to have been a reaction set in, since the E. P. Hammond meetings for says, the letter of the church to the association, there has not been in years so much worldliness in the church as during the past winter. The prayer meetings of the church are poorly attended, the congregation small and the financial obligations against the church have increased somewhat The Rev. Mr. Wright resigns in November 1878, and Rev. R. E. Williams is at once called to the pastorate. He remained but six months. Of this short pastorate little is said. He was greatly admired as a preacher and as a cultured Christian gentleman. No additions are made to the church and the financial obligations of the church continue to grow. On the first of January,1880, the Rev. R. B. Montgomery became pastor of this church His, too, was a short pastorate, lasting only thirteen months, but remarkable in this, that he succeeding in securing pledges at home and abroad sufficient to meet the entire mortgage debt and interest. And for this he richly merited and received the heartfelt gratitude of the church and society, a vote to this effect being recorded on the books of the church In May, 1881, Rev. John Gilchrist became pastor. Under this pastorate there was some friction in the church. It led to the exclusion of one or more members and the withdrawal of several others. The pastor at once resigned, and closed another pastorate of less than two years. The church was then supplied for a few months by Rev. J. J. Phelps. A call was given Rev. Seward Robson. Accepted and he became the pastor of the church December 1st, 1882 He remained as pastor a little over four years. Thirty-nine were added to the church by baptism. During this pastorate, in 1885, the district secretary of the state convention Rev. Mr. Brooks, assisted the pastor in evangelist services for several weeks There had been a continuous running behind in the pastor's salary, and at the time of his resignation the church was obligated to their pastor to the amount of over $750. In June the Rev. James Grant, a student in the Rochester seminary, is called as a sup ply. This is the year '88, and on May 1st, 1889, the Rev. S. J. White becomes pastor. Though but few conversions are reported and something in bene-volences ouside of the home field, yet few the churches and fow the pastors that made the sacrifices that this church must have made, and the pastor as well, to leave on record the fact that nearly $1,400 had been raised during the first year of Mr. White's pastorate, the Rev. Seward Robinson, the former pastor, paid in full, though the church was owing him more than $400 when this pastorate began. And so at the associational gathering held in September, 1890, the church reports that they are practically out of debt, but in their present condition, unable longer to meet the running expenses of the church, and appealing to the State and county missionary committees to know what can be done. On March 27th, 1891, it was voted to have the secre-

tary of the Baptist State convention visit the field and hold a missionary convention with this church. Such a convention was held and was thought to be of real profit to the church. The Rev. S. H. White's pastorate ended in July, 1891, he having been pastor of the church a little over two years The church was again without a pastor and preaching was only sustained part of the time, and this by supplies. But on November 30th, 1891, a meeting is called for the purpose of deciding upon and calling a pastor, so advised by the State convention and the missionary committee of the Ontario Baptist as-sociation. At this meeting it is de-cided to extend a call to the Rev. E. C. Long, then of Manchester, N. Y. Such a call is extended, but he declines to accept. Another meeting is called for January 12th to take under considera-tion the advisability of extending a call to Rev. J. Cody, and by a vote of the church it is decided not to extend the call. And on January 28, 1892, a third and similar meeting is called to take into consideration the advisability of extending a call to the Rev. S. M. Newland, then of Clifton Springs, N. Y A vote is taken, and in the letter sent notifying him of the decision of the church, it was stated that the vote was unanimous in extending such a call, and, whether wisely or unwisely, the present pastor of the church ac-cepted it, commencing his labors April 1st, 1892. Of this pastorate we need to say little. It is not finished as yet But as it already covers a period of nearly twelve years, already more than double that of any other in the history of the church, and as it is a history of church life you have asked for in this paper, a brief summary of the present pastor's work with this church cannot be out of place. During these twelve years it has not been all sunshine. We have had some cloudy and dark days of discouragement; and yet on the whole it has been a happy, contented and we trust, in some small degree, a prosper-ous pastorate thus far. When this pastorate began the church records gave a membership of 110. The pres ent pastor has baptised into the church fellowship, 132; 70 have been received by letter. The present membership of the church is 238, the largest number, with the exception of the one year, 1843, ever reported by this church. In briefly summing up the history of the First Baptist church of Seneca Falls, N. Y., beginning in 1828 we find that the church has a history of seventy-five years. Twenty three pastors The shortest pastorate was that of Rev. Mr. Williams, lasting only six months; the longest tha' of the present pastor, now nearly twelve years; the next longest, that of the Rev. Wm. R. Wright, a little over five years. We give the names and length of each pastorate: 1, Orsamus Allen, 3 years 9 months; 2, Henry C. Vogell, 2 years 9 months; 3, John Jeffres, 2 years; 4 Zenas Freeman, 3 years; 5, E R. Pinney, 2 years 1 month; 6, Nathan Baker, 4 years; 7, W H. Hall, 1 year 2 months; 8, Wm. Frary. 1 year; 9, J. B. Pitman, 2 years; 10. Wm. Legget; 1 year 2 months; 11, Ira Smith. 8 months; 12, C. C. Hart, 7 months: 13, Wm. Rees, 3 years; 14, Ferris Scott, 5 years 4 months: 15. Ira Bennett, 2 years 10 months; 16 B. F. Garfield, 2 years 3 months; 17, Wm. R. Wright, 5 years 3 months; 18, R. E. Wililams, 6 months; 19, B. R. Montgomery, 1 year; month 20, John Gilchristt, 1 year 11 months; 21, Seward Robinson 4 years 4 months; 22, S. H. White, 2 years 3 months; 23. S M. Newland, 11 years 9 months: years of pastoral service. 64 years 8 months; average 2 years 10 months. Nearly eleven years of its history the church has been without a regular pastor. There has been no uniform salary, and it has been from $250 to $1,000. Not far from 700 persons have been baptised into the church during its history and about 400 have been received by letter. There were 14 constituent members, so not far from 1,100 persons have been connected with this church during its history. The largest number, as already stated, in the membership of the church was at the close of 1843, when the church reported a membership of 242; the smallest number since the first partorate, 69, in the year 1873. To-day the church reports 238 members, the Sunday school the largest since the year 1842, or within a period of more than sixty years; free from debt, not by any means satisfied or accomplishing what she should, but united and a measure of prosperity attending the efforts of pastor and people, for which we give praise and thanksgiving to Almighty God, who we believe has led us thus far, and we look forward hopefully into the future.